GRIMWOOD'S DAUGHTER

BY JAN S. STRNAD & KEVIN NOWLAN

www.IDWPUBLISHING.com

GRIMWOOD'S DAUGHTER

Written by
JAN S. STRNAD

Illustrated by
KEVIN NOWLAN

Original Edits by
GARY GROTH

Collection Edits by
JUSTIN EISINGER

Collection Design by
CHRIS MOWRY

Special thanks to Julie Strnad, Deanne Nowlan,
Scott Dunbier, Jimmy Palmiotti, Phil Felix, Marc Brown,
Richard DeDominicis, Scott Reno, Richard Donnelly,
J. R. R. Tolkien (for making elves cool), Wendy Pini (for
making them cool again), and the gang at Fantagraphics.

ISBN: 978-1-60010-504-3
12 11 10 09   1 2 3 4

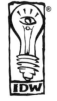

www.IDWPUBLISHING.com

IDW Publi
Opera
Ted Adams, Chief Executive O
Greg Goldstein, Chief Operating O
Matthew Ruzicka, CPA, Chief Financial O
Alan Payne, VP of
Lorelei Bunjes, Dir. of Digital Ser
AnnaMaria White, Marketing & PR Ma
Marci Hubbard, Executive Ass
Alonzo Simon, Shipping Ma
Angela Loggins, Staff Accou

Edi
Chris Ryall, Publisher/Editor-in-
Scott Dunbier, Editor, Special Pro
Andy Schmidt, Senior E
Justin Eisinger, E
Kris Oprisko, Editor/Foreig
Denton J. Tipton, E
Tom Waltz, E
Mariah Huehner, Associate E
Carlos Guzman, Editorial Ass

De
Robbie Robbins, EVP/Sr. Graphic
Neil Uyetake, Art Di
Chris Mowry, Graphic
Amauri Osorio, Graphic
Gilberto Lazcano, Production Ass

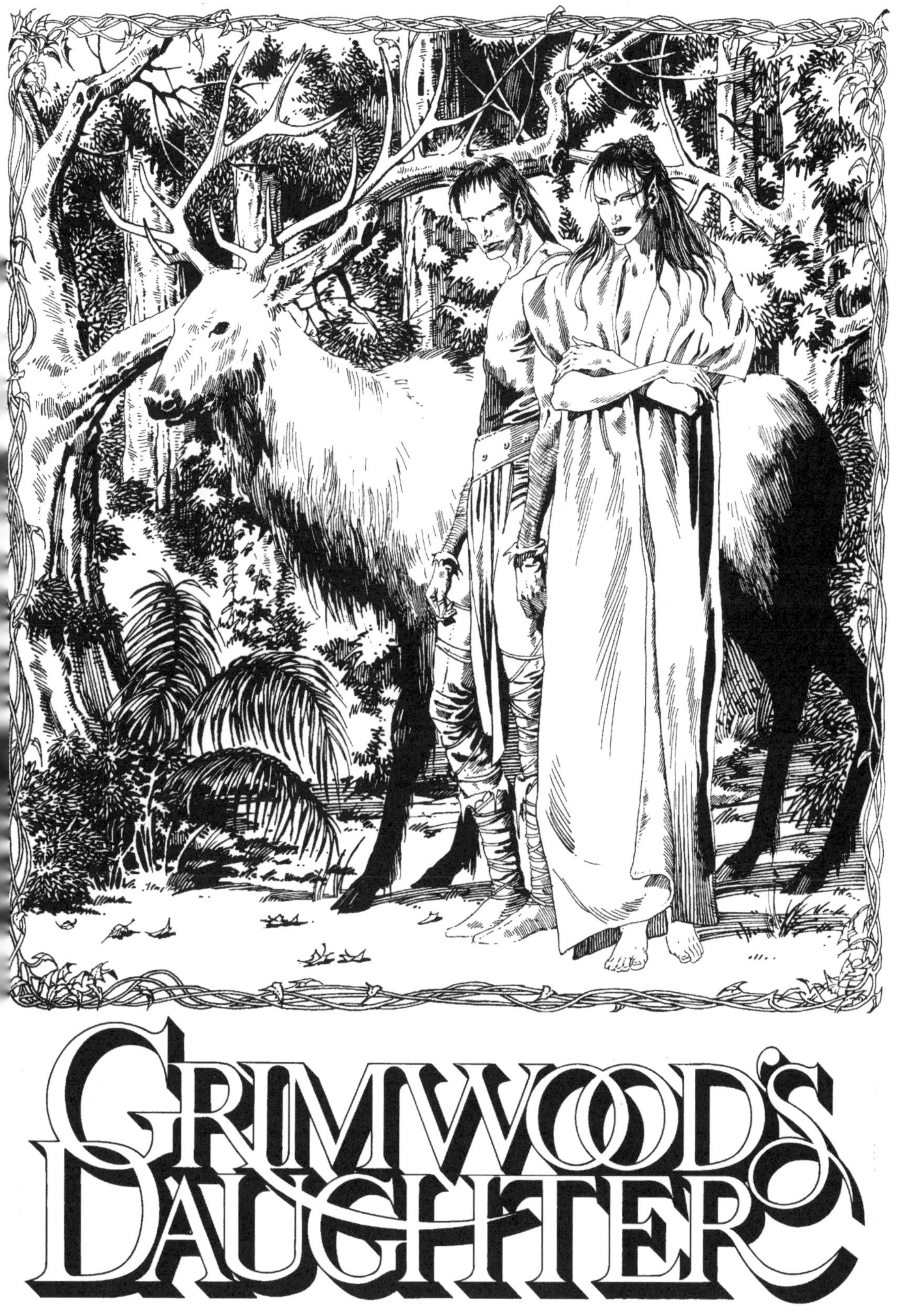

GRIMWOOD'S DAUGHTER

Y JAN S. STRNAD & KEVIN NOWLAN

THE ELFIN WAR WITH MAN IS DRAWING TO A CLOSE.
TIROL OF GRIMWOOD HAS RIDDEN FAR TO SOLICIT THE HELP OF A RIVAL CLAN, ONLY TO FIND THAT HE HAS ARRIVED TOO LATE.

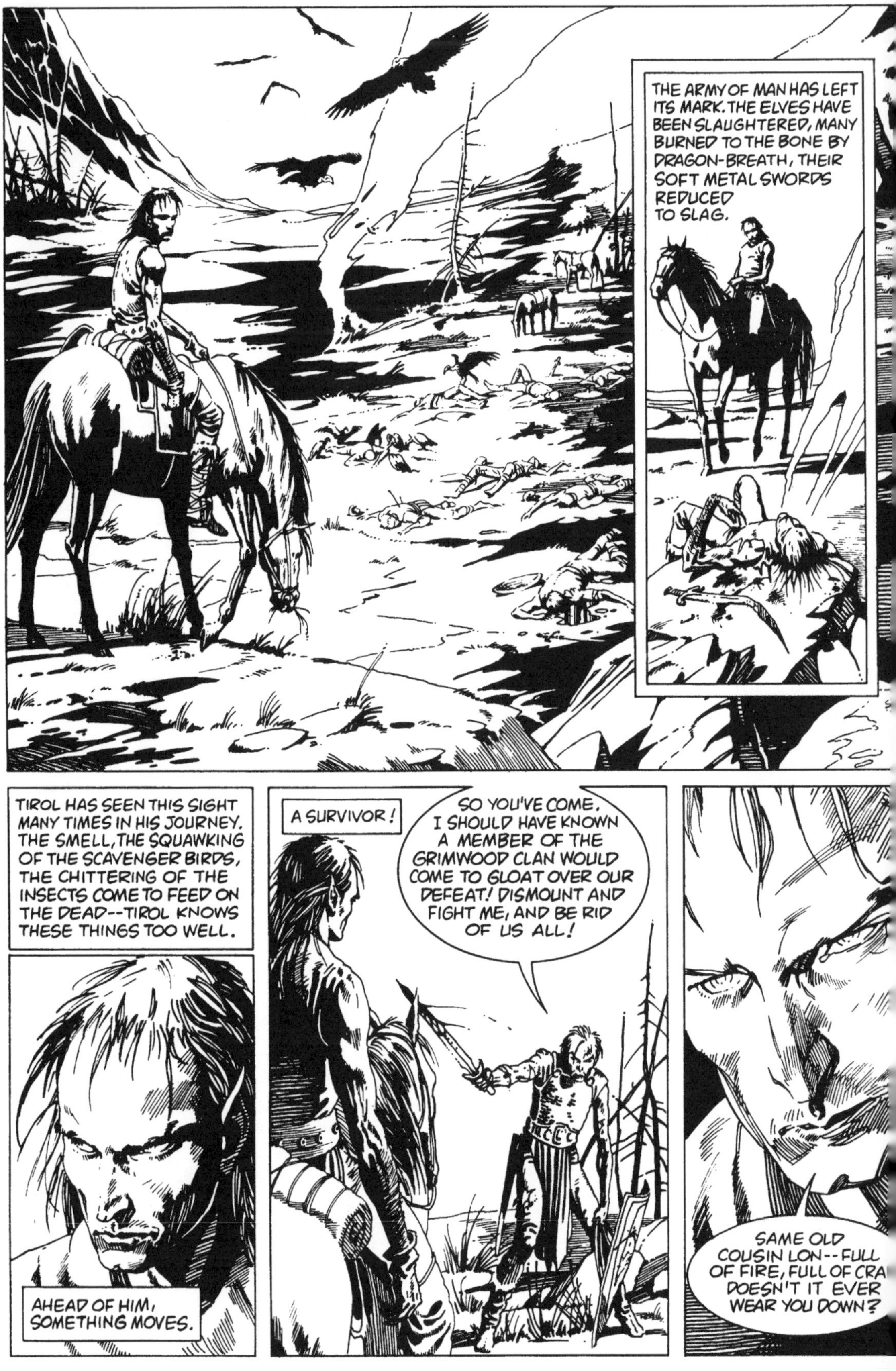
THE ARMY OF MAN HAS LEFT ITS MARK. THE ELVES HAVE BEEN SLAUGHTERED, MANY BURNED TO THE BONE BY DRAGON-BREATH, THEIR SOFT METAL SWORDS REDUCED TO SLAG.
TIROL HAS SEEN THIS SIGHT MANY TIMES IN HIS JOURNEY. THE SMELL, THE SQUAWKING OF THE SCAVENGER BIRDS, THE CHITTERING OF THE INSECTS COME TO FEED ON THE DEAD--TIROL KNOWS THESE THINGS TOO WELL.
AHEAD OF HIM, SOMETHING MOVES.
A SURVIVOR!
SO YOU'VE COME. I SHOULD HAVE KNOWN A MEMBER OF THE GRIMWOOD CLAN WOULD COME TO GLOAT OVER OUR DEFEAT! DISMOUNT AND FIGHT ME, AND BE RID OF US ALL!
SAME OLD COUSIN LON--FULL OF FIRE, FULL OF CRA
DOESN'T IT EVER WEAR YOU DOWN?

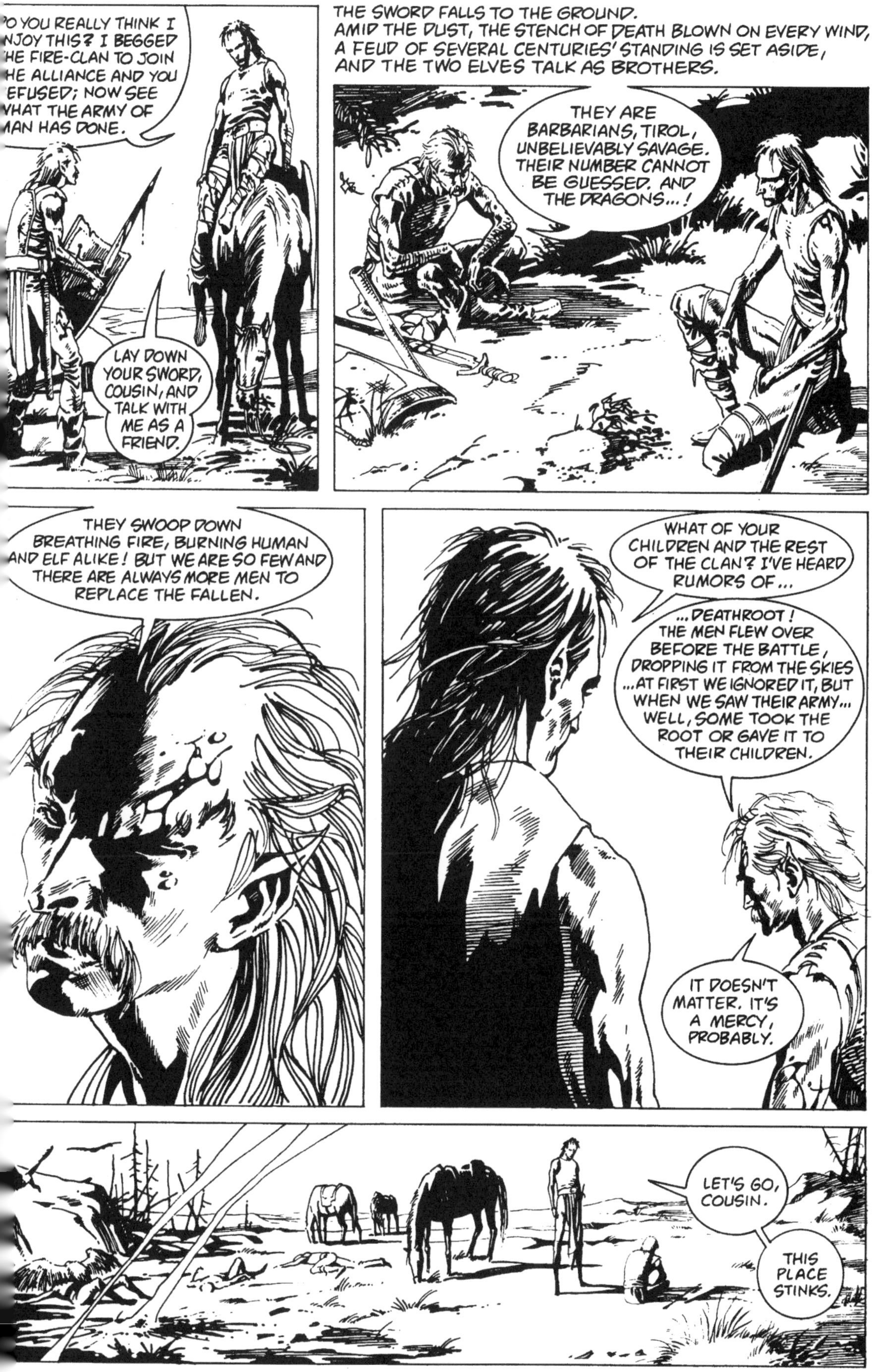
O YOU REALLY THINK I NJOY THIS? I BEGGED HE FIRE-CLAN TO JOIN HE ALLIANCE AND YOU EFUSED; NOW SEE WHAT THE ARMY OF MAN HAS DONE.
LAY DOWN YOUR SWORD, COUSIN, AND TALK WITH ME AS A FRIEND.
THE SWORD FALLS TO THE GROUND. AMID THE DUST, THE STENCH OF DEATH BLOWN ON EVERY WIND, A FEUD OF SEVERAL CENTURIES' STANDING IS SET ASIDE, AND THE TWO ELVES TALK AS BROTHERS.
THEY ARE BARBARIANS, TIROL, UNBELIEVABLY SAVAGE. THEIR NUMBER CANNOT BE GUESSED. AND THE DRAGONS...!
THEY SWOOP DOWN BREATHING FIRE, BURNING HUMAN AND ELF ALIKE! BUT WE ARE SO FEW AND THERE ARE ALWAYS MORE MEN TO REPLACE THE FALLEN.
WHAT OF YOUR CHILDREN AND THE REST OF THE CLAN? I'VE HEARD RUMORS OF...
...DEATHROOT! THE MEN FLEW OVER BEFORE THE BATTLE, DROPPING IT FROM THE SKIES ...AT FIRST WE IGNORED IT, BUT WHEN WE SAW THEIR ARMY... WELL, SOME TOOK THE ROOT OR GAVE IT TO THEIR CHILDREN.
IT DOESN'T MATTER. IT'S A MERCY, PROBABLY.
LET'S GO, COUSIN.
THIS PLACE STINKS.

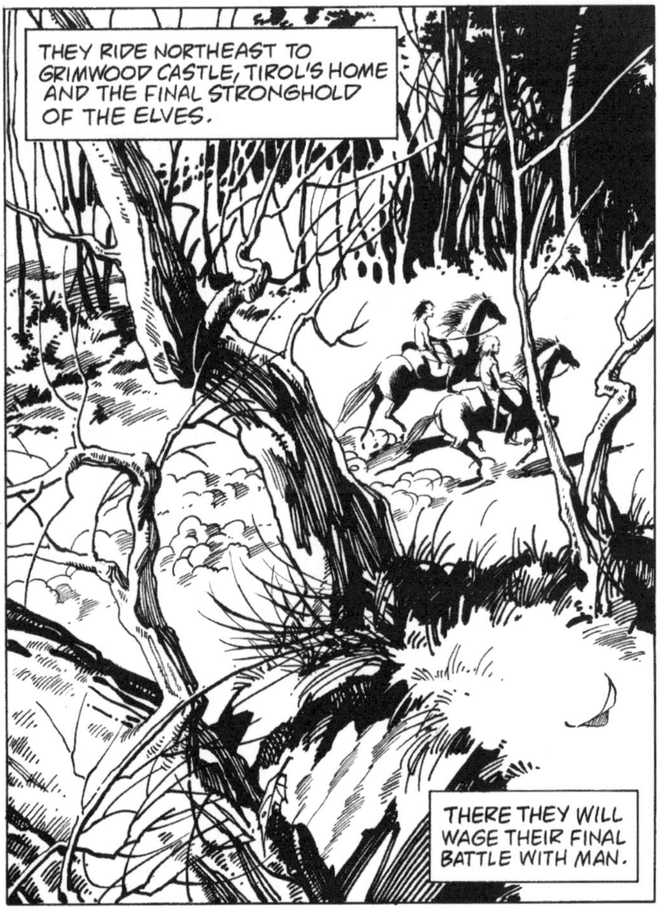
THEY RIDE NORTHEAST TO GRIMWOOD CASTLE, TIROL'S HOME AND THE FINAL STRONGHOLD OF THE ELVES.
THERE THEY WILL WAGE THEIR FINAL BATTLE WITH MAN.

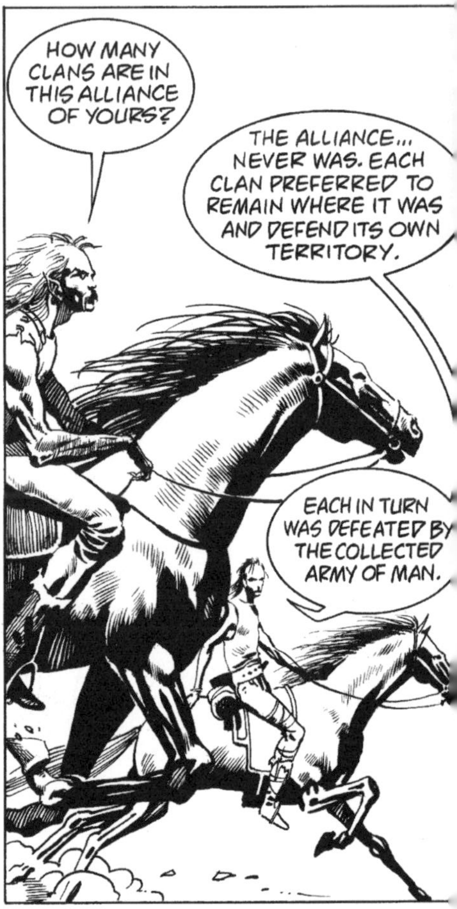
HOW MANY CLANS ARE IN THIS ALLIANCE OF YOURS?
THE ALLIANCE... NEVER WAS. EACH CLAN PREFERRED TO REMAIN WHERE IT WAS AND DEFEND ITS OWN TERRITORY.
EACH IN TURN WAS DEFEATED BY THE COLLECTED ARMY OF MAN.

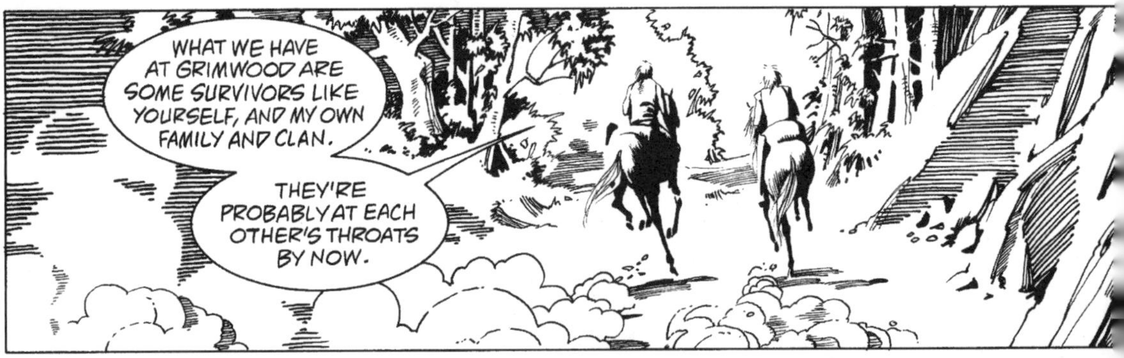
WHAT WE HAVE AT GRIMWOOD ARE SOME SURVIVORS LIKE YOURSELF, AND MY OWN FAMILY AND CLAN.
THEY'RE PROBABLY AT EACH OTHER'S THROATS BY NOW.

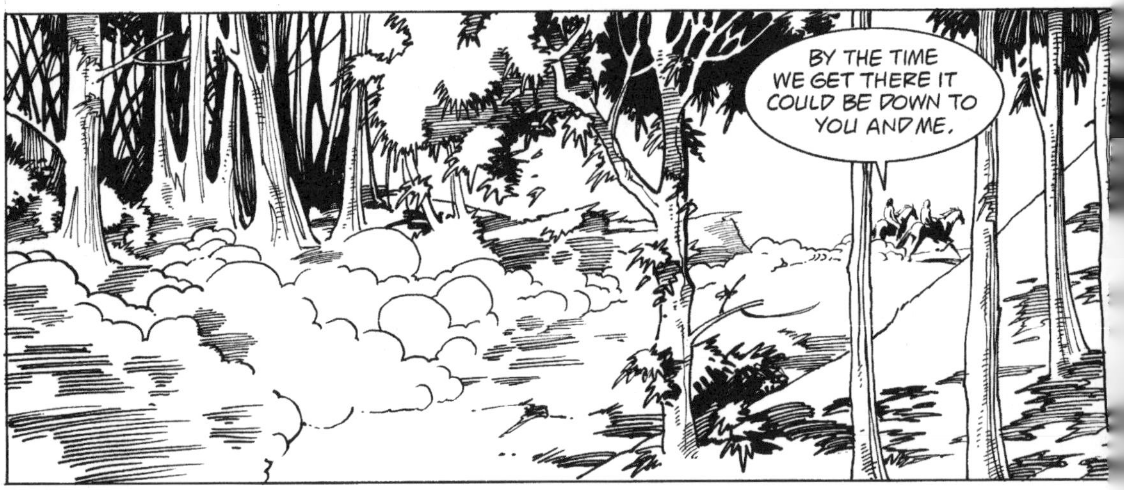
BY THE TIME WE GET THERE IT COULD BE DOWN TO YOU AND ME.

ITUATED ON THE EDGE OF THE KNOWN, HABITABLE WORLD, GRIMWOOD CASTLE ONCE TOOD APART FROM THE ANCIENT FOREST FOR WHICH IT WAS NAMED. OVER THE CENTURIES THE FOREST NEXORABLY FOLDED THE CASTLE IN ITS LEAFY EMBRACE, UNTIL NOW, THE TWO HAVE BECOME ONE.

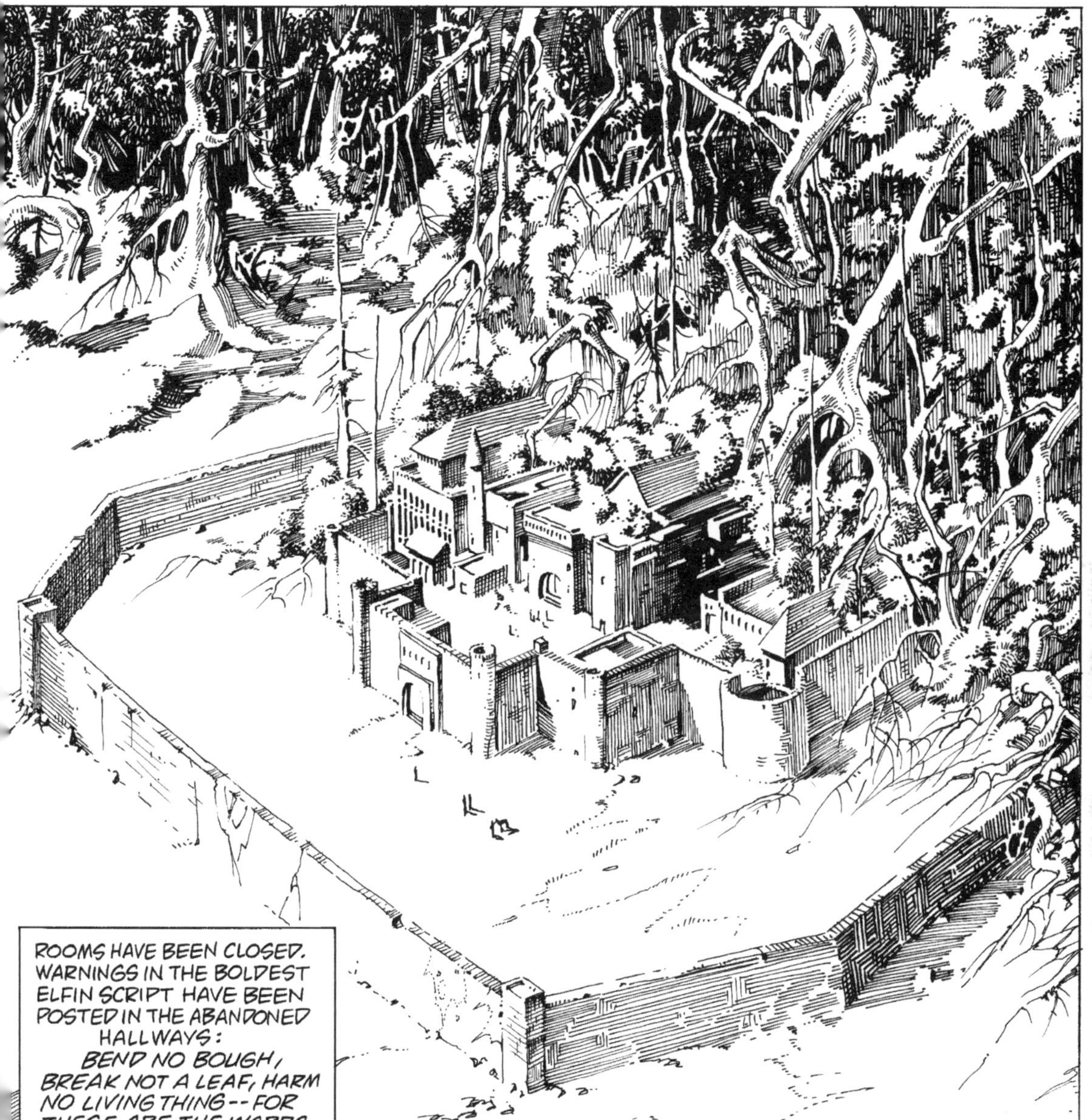
ROOMS HAVE BEEN CLOSED. WARNINGS IN THE BOLDEST ELFIN SCRIPT HAVE BEEN POSTED IN THE ABANDONED HALLWAYS:
BEND NO BOUGH, BREAK NOT A LEAF, HARM NO LIVING THING--FOR THESE ARE THE WARDS OF THE SPIRITS OF GRIMWOOD, SPIRITS WITH NO HEARTS IN WHICH TO HARBOR LOVE FOR ELVES.

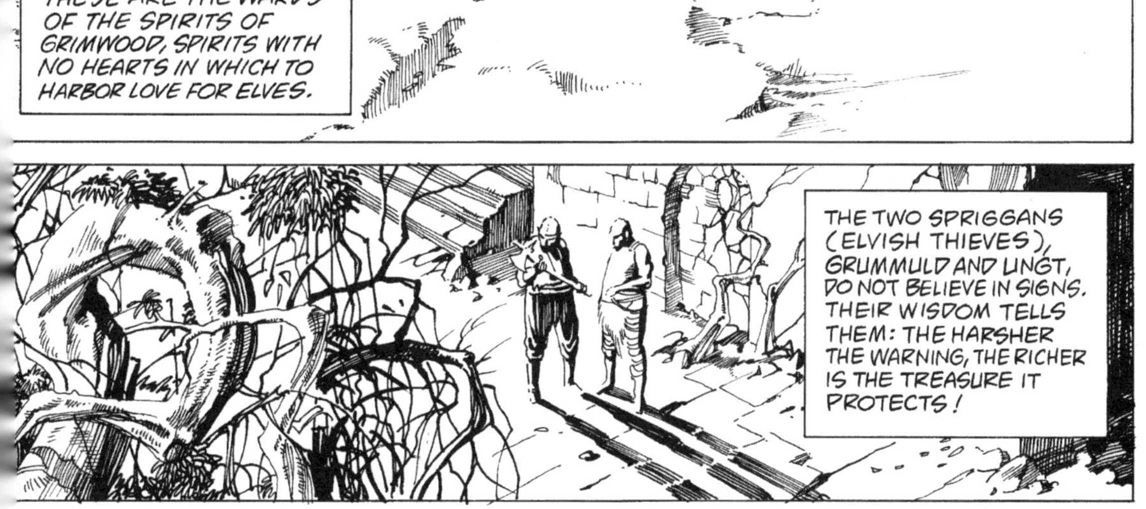
THE TWO SPRIGGANS (ELVISH THIEVES), GRUMMULD AND UNGT, DO NOT BELIEVE IN SIGNS. THEIR WISDOM TELLS THEM: THE HARSHER THE WARNING, THE RICHER IS THE TREASURE IT PROTECTS!

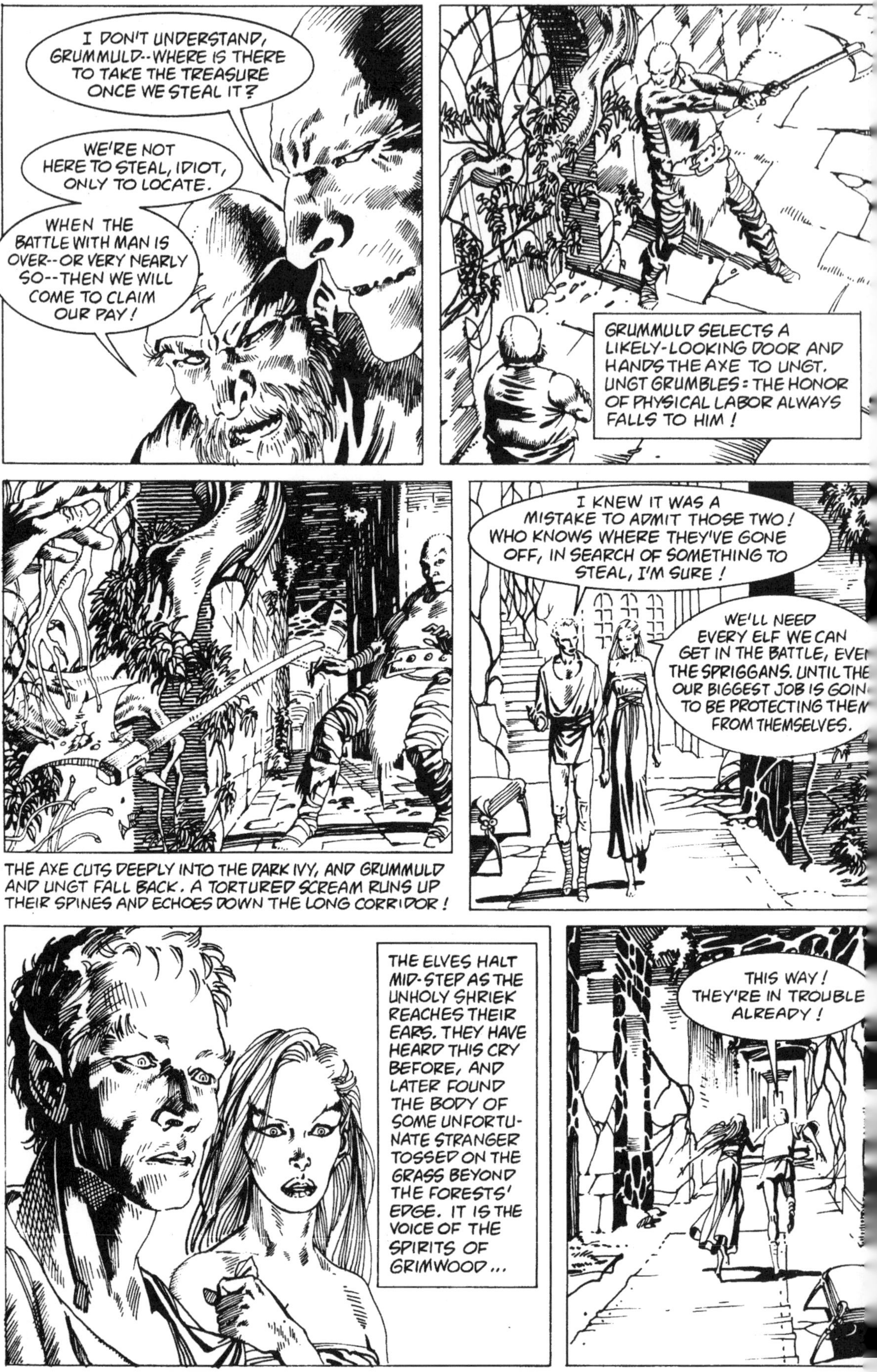
I DON'T UNDERSTAND, GRUMMULD--WHERE IS THERE TO TAKE THE TREASURE ONCE WE STEAL IT?
WE'RE NOT HERE TO STEAL, IDIOT, ONLY TO LOCATE.
WHEN THE BATTLE WITH MAN IS OVER--OR VERY NEARLY SO--THEN WE WILL COME TO CLAIM OUR PAY!
GRUMMULD SELECTS A LIKELY-LOOKING DOOR AND HANDS THE AXE TO UNGT. UNGT GRUMBLES: THE HONOR OF PHYSICAL LABOR ALWAYS FALLS TO HIM!
THE AXE CUTS DEEPLY INTO THE DARK IVY, AND GRUMMULD AND UNGT FALL BACK. A TORTURED SCREAM RUNS UP THEIR SPINES AND ECHOES DOWN THE LONG CORRIDOR!
I KNEW IT WAS A MISTAKE TO ADMIT THOSE TWO! WHO KNOWS WHERE THEY'VE GONE OFF, IN SEARCH OF SOMETHING TO STEAL, I'M SURE!
WE'LL NEED EVERY ELF WE CAN GET IN THE BATTLE, EVE THE SPRIGGANS. UNTIL THE OUR BIGGEST JOB IS GOIN TO BE PROTECTING THEM FROM THEMSELVES.
THE ELVES HALT MID-STEP AS THE UNHOLY SHRIEK REACHES THEIR EARS. THEY HAVE HEARD THIS CRY BEFORE, AND LATER FOUND THE BODY OF SOME UNFORTU-NATE STRANGER TOSSED ON THE GRASS BEYOND THE FORESTS' EDGE. IT IS THE VOICE OF THE SPIRITS OF GRIMWOOD...
THIS WAY! THEY'RE IN TROUBLE ALREADY!

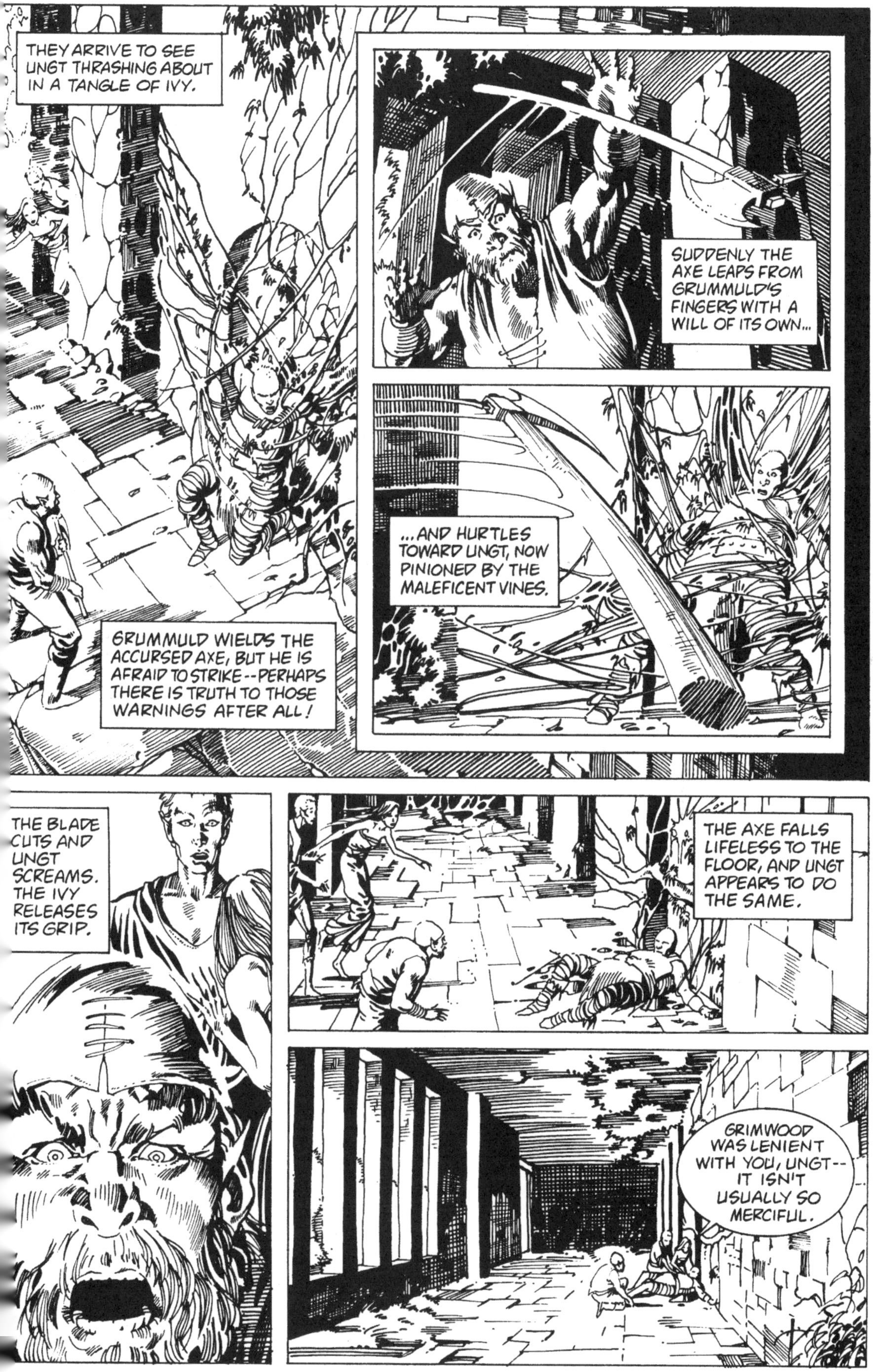
THEY ARRIVE TO SEE UNGT THRASHING ABOUT IN A TANGLE OF IVY.
GRUMMULD WIELDS THE ACCURSED AXE, BUT HE IS AFRAID TO STRIKE--PERHAPS THERE IS TRUTH TO THOSE WARNINGS AFTER ALL!
SUDDENLY THE AXE LEAPS FROM GRUMMULD'S FINGERS WITH A WILL OF ITS OWN...
...AND HURTLES TOWARD UNGT, NOW PINIONED BY THE MALEFICENT VINES.
THE BLADE CUTS AND UNGT SCREAMS. THE IVY RELEASES ITS GRIP.
THE AXE FALLS LIFELESS TO THE FLOOR, AND UNGT APPEARS TO DO THE SAME.
GRIMWOOD WAS LENIENT WITH YOU, UNGT-- IT ISN'T USUALLY SO MERCIFUL.

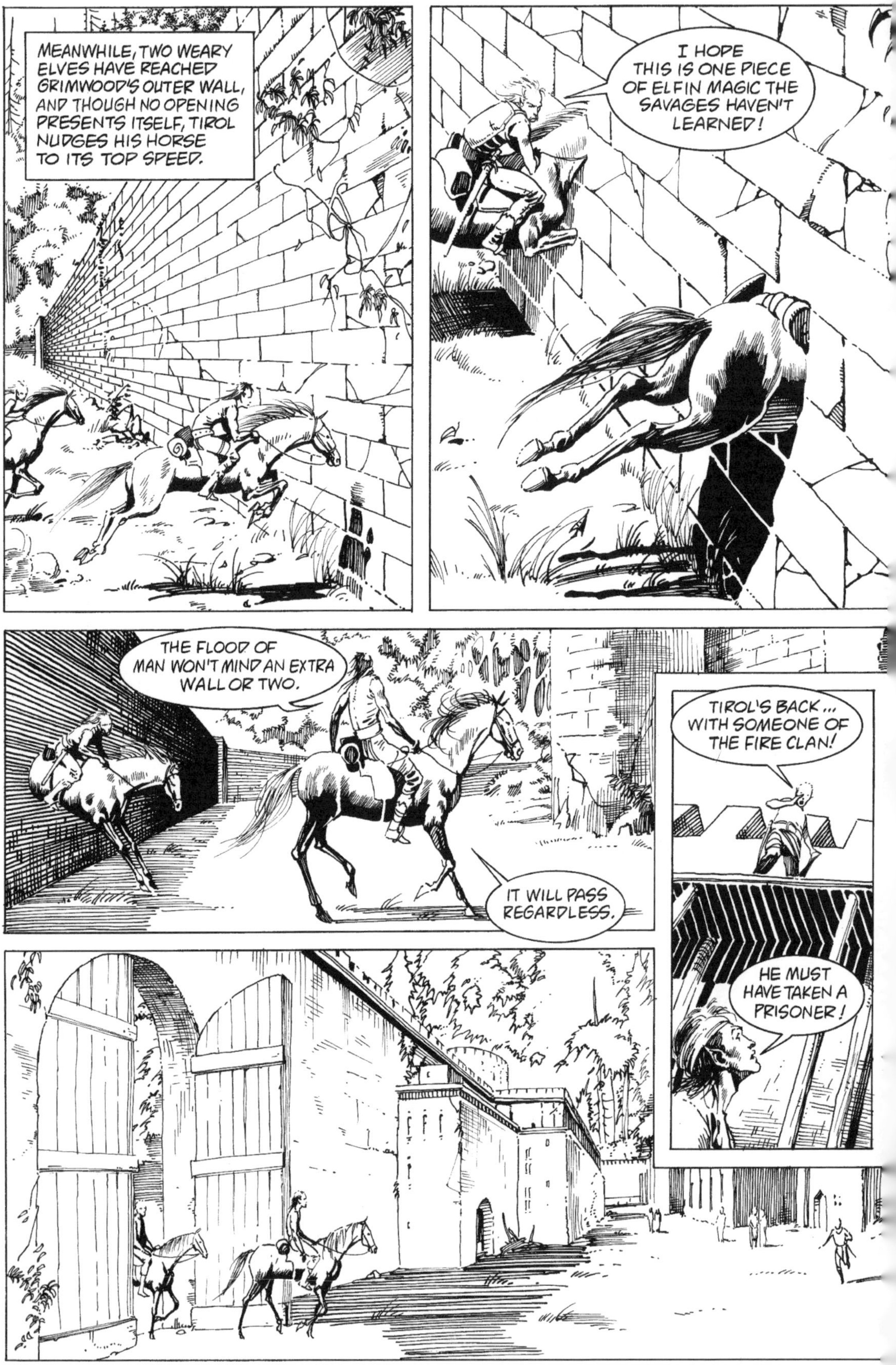
MEANWHILE, TWO WEARY ELVES HAVE REACHED GRIMWOOD'S OUTER WALL, AND THOUGH NO OPENING PRESENTS ITSELF, TIROL NUDGES HIS HORSE TO ITS TOP SPEED.
I HOPE THIS IS ONE PIECE OF ELFIN MAGIC THE SAVAGES HAVEN'T LEARNED!
THE FLOOD OF MAN WON'T MIND AN EXTRA WALL OR TWO.
IT WILL PASS REGARDLESS.
TIROL'S BACK... WITH SOMEONE OF THE FIRE CLAN!
HE MUST HAVE TAKEN A PRISONER!

SOME DEEP, UNRECOGNIZED PART OF TIROL HAD DARED DREAM OF A CASTLE BURSTING WITH ELVES, OF TENTS ERECTED IN THE COURTYARDS TO HOUSE THOSE THE CASTLE COULD NOT HOLD. HE BECO AWARE OF THIS UNSPOKEN DREAM ONLY AS THE DREAM DIES, FOR THE YARD IS ALL BUT EMPTY.

UCH TO THE SURPRISE OF THE VISITING ELVES, TIROL INTRODUCES HIS COUSIN LON AS AN ALLY,
ND LON IS GREETED WARMLY BY TIROL'S SISTER, SHARDA, AND HER HUSBAND, DOSKEN.

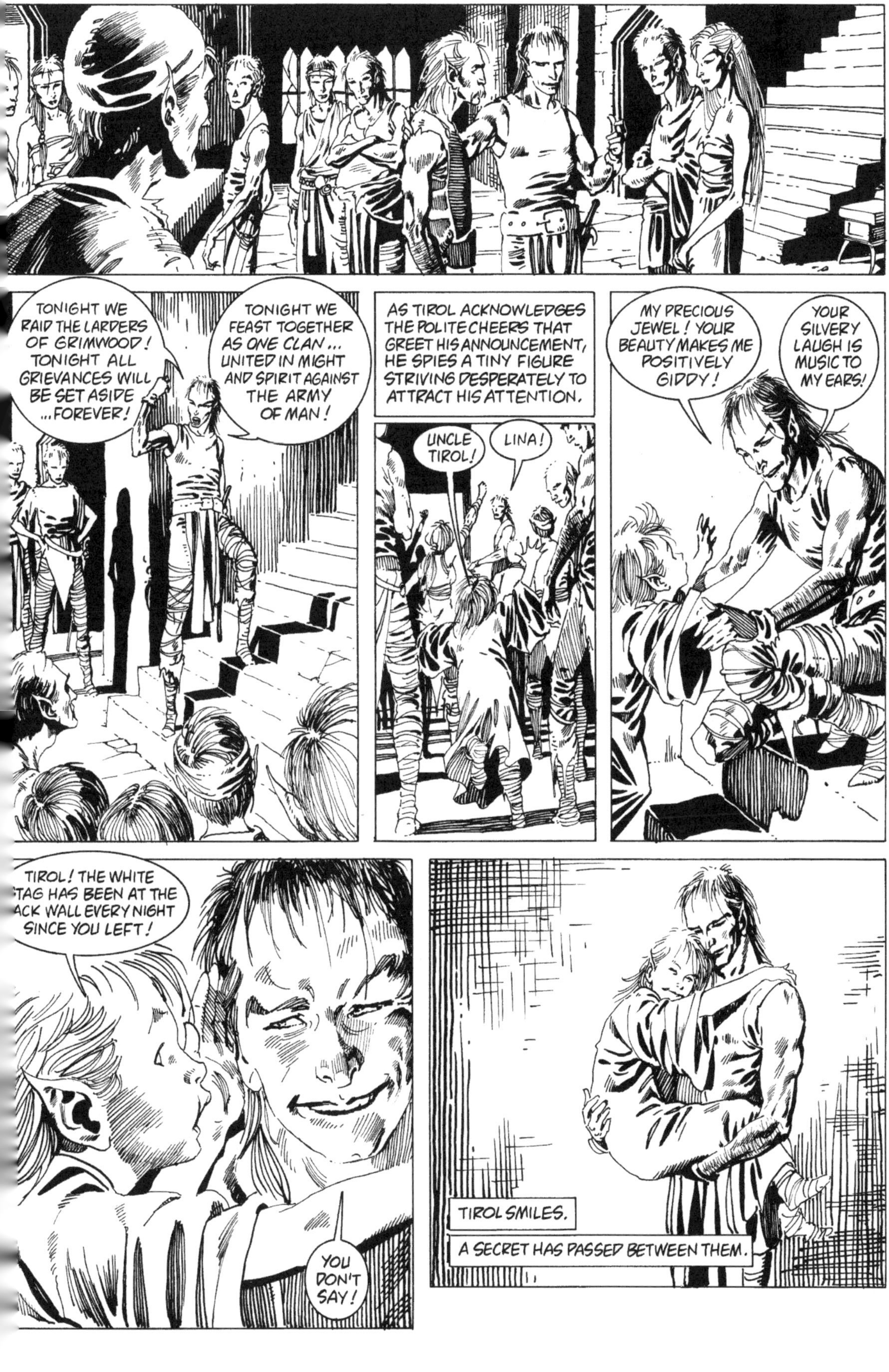
TONIGHT WE RAID THE LARDERS OF GRIMWOOD! TONIGHT ALL GRIEVANCES WILL BE SET ASIDE ...FOREVER!
TONIGHT WE FEAST TOGETHER AS ONE CLAN... UNITED IN MIGHT AND SPIRIT AGAINST THE ARMY OF MAN!
AS TIROL ACKNOWLEDGES THE POLITE CHEERS THAT GREET HIS ANNOUNCEMENT, HE SPIES A TINY FIGURE STRIVING DESPERATELY TO ATTRACT HIS ATTENTION.
UNCLE TIROL!
LINA!
MY PRECIOUS JEWEL! YOUR BEAUTY MAKES ME POSITIVELY GIDDY!
YOUR SILVERY LAUGH IS MUSIC TO MY EARS!
TIROL! THE WHITE TAG HAS BEEN AT THE ACK WALL EVERY NIGHT SINCE YOU LEFT!
YOU DON'T SAY!
TIROL SMILES.
A SECRET HAS PASSED BETWEEN THEM.

GRIMWOOD'S DAUGHTER

CHAPTER TW

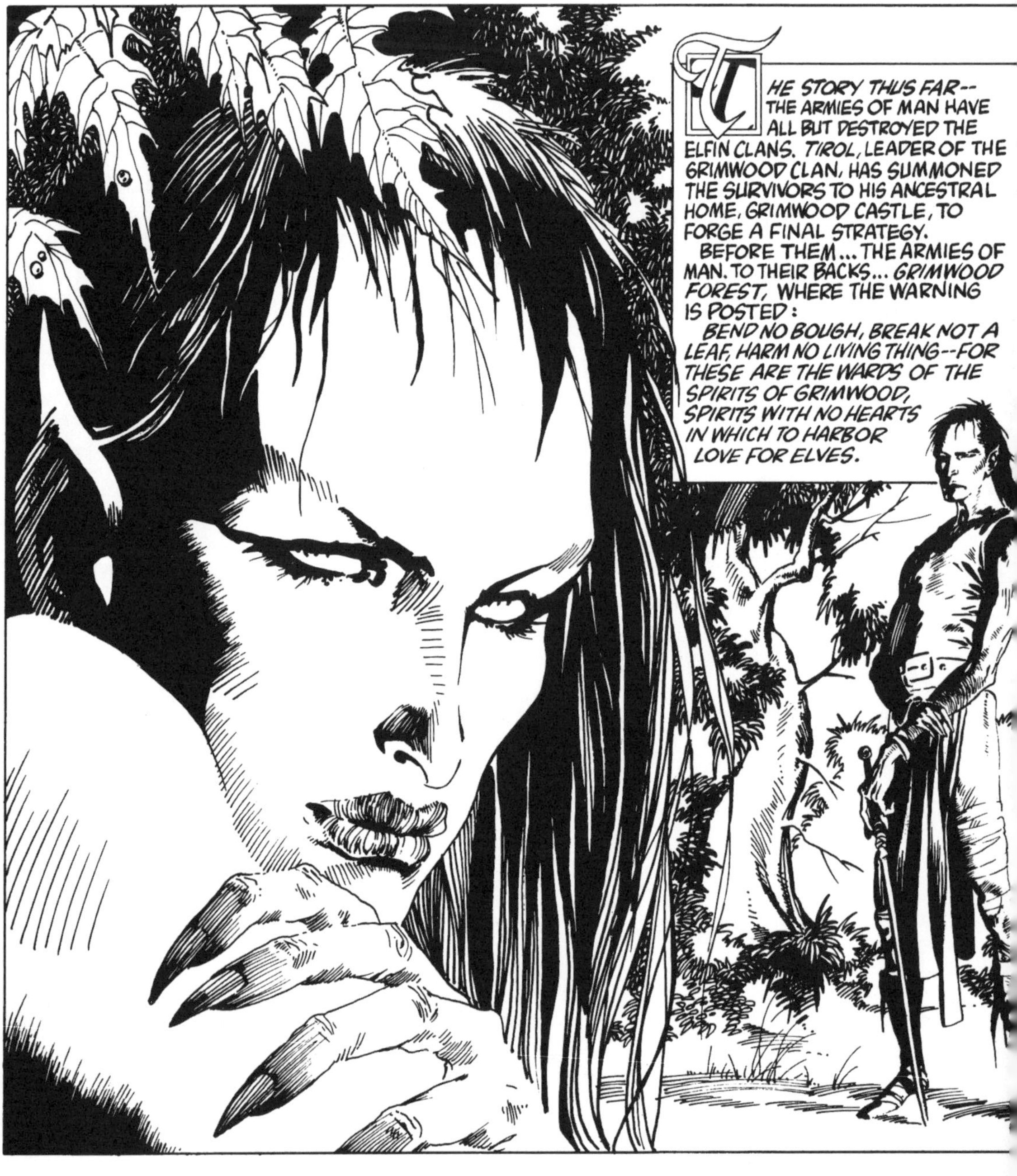
THE STORY THUS FAR-- THE ARMIES OF MAN HAVE ALL BUT DESTROYED THE ELFIN CLANS. TIROL, LEADER OF THE GRIMWOOD CLAN, HAS SUMMONED THE SURVIVORS TO HIS ANCESTRAL HOME, GRIMWOOD CASTLE, TO FORGE A FINAL STRATEGY.
BEFORE THEM... THE ARMIES OF MAN. TO THEIR BACKS... GRIMWOOD FOREST, WHERE THE WARNING IS POSTED:
BEND NO BOUGH, BREAK NOT A LEAF, HARM NO LIVING THING--FOR THESE ARE THE WARDS OF THE SPIRITS OF GRIMWOOD, SPIRITS WITH NO HEARTS IN WHICH TO HARBOR LOVE FOR ELVES.

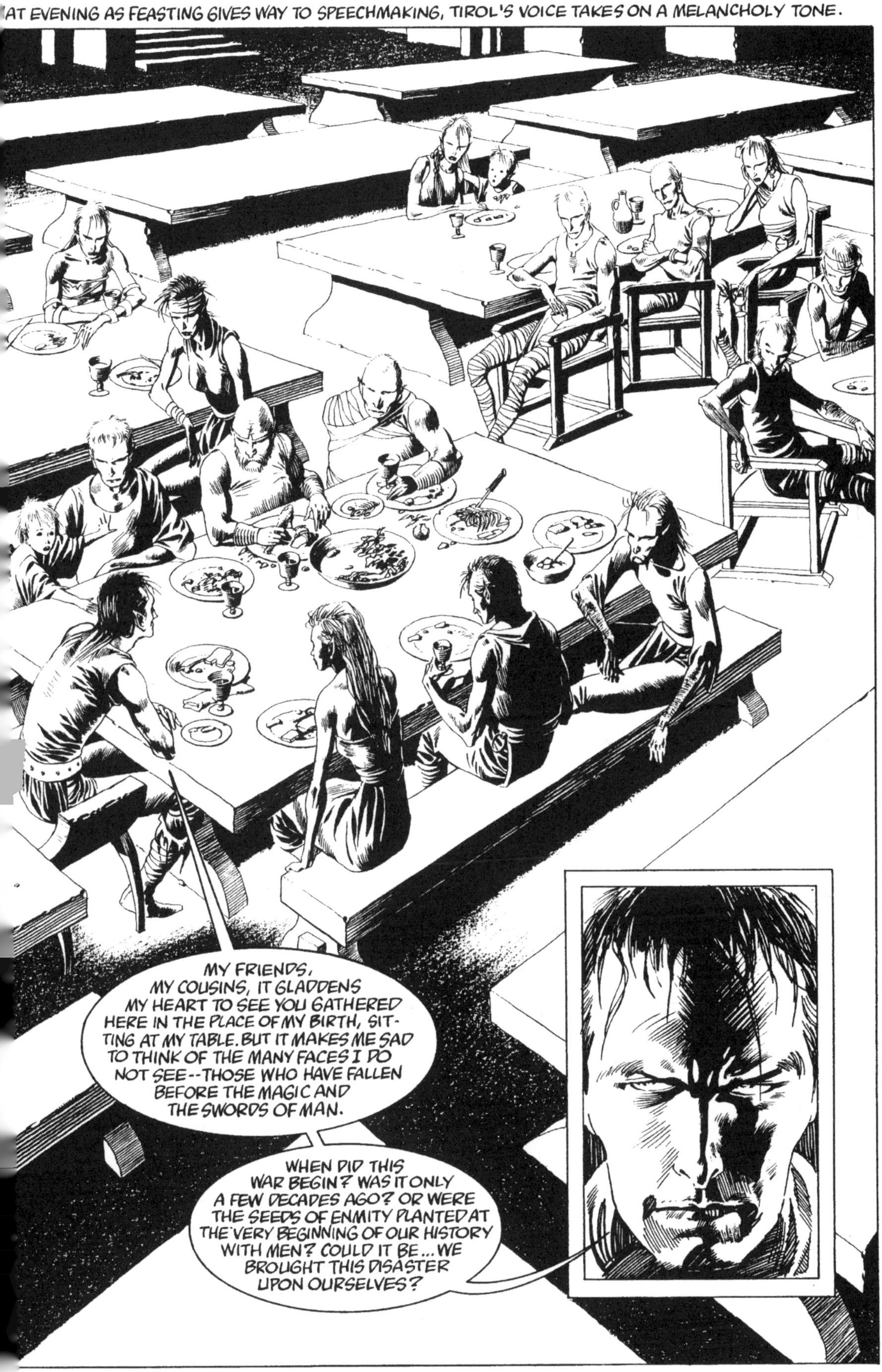
AT EVENING AS FEASTING GIVES WAY TO SPEECHMAKING, TIROL'S VOICE TAKES ON A MELANCHOLY TONE.
MY FRIENDS, MY COUSINS, IT GLADDENS MY HEART TO SEE YOU GATHERED HERE IN THE PLACE OF MY BIRTH, SITTING AT MY TABLE. BUT IT MAKES ME SAD TO THINK OF THE MANY FACES I DO NOT SEE--THOSE WHO HAVE FALLEN BEFORE THE MAGIC AND THE SWORDS OF MAN.
WHEN DID THIS WAR BEGIN? WAS IT ONLY A FEW DECADES AGO? OR WERE THE SEEDS OF ENMITY PLANTED AT THE VERY BEGINNING OF OUR HISTORY WITH MEN? COULD IT BE... WE BROUGHT THIS DISASTER UPON OURSELVES?

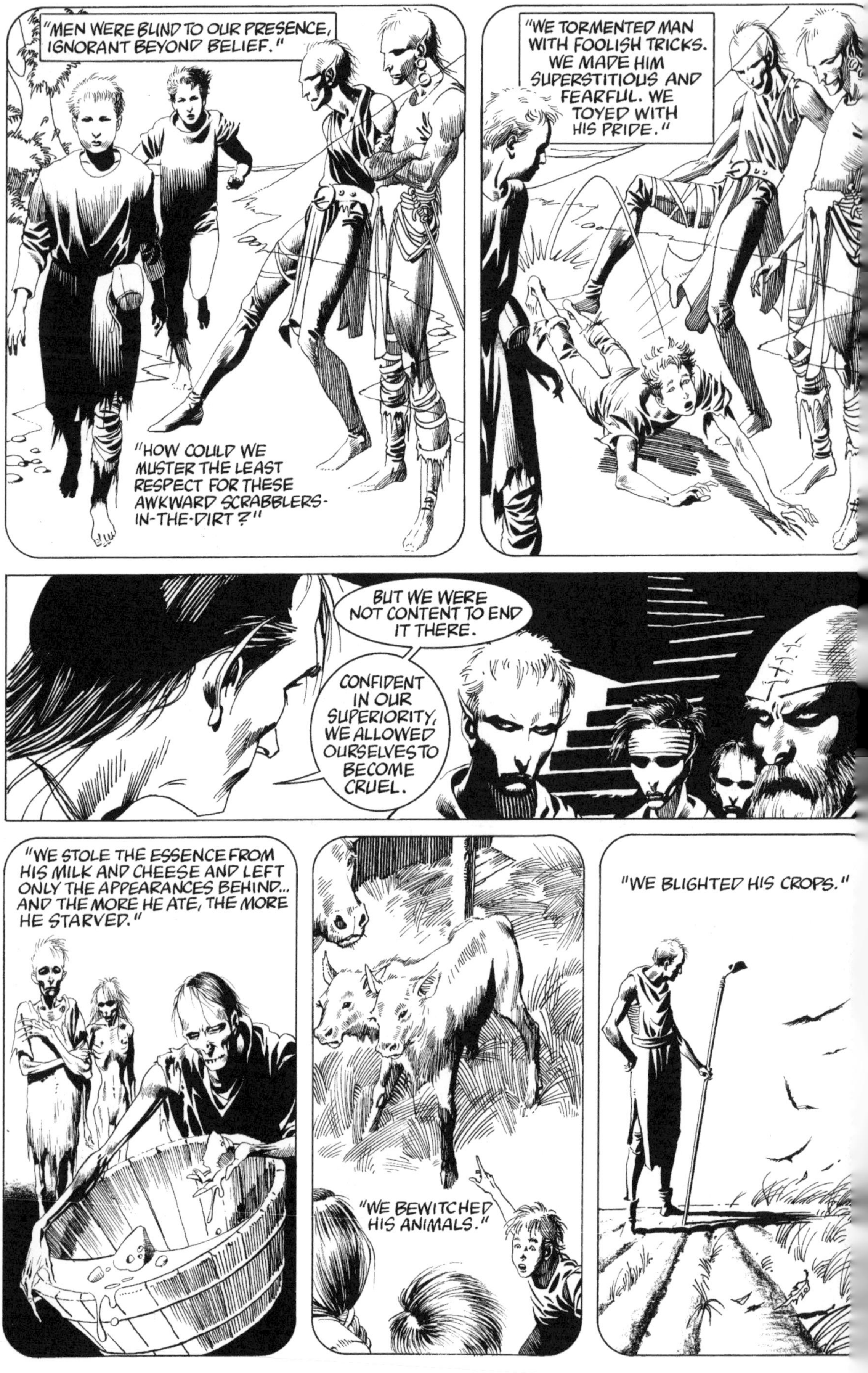
"MEN WERE BLIND TO OUR PRESENCE, IGNORANT BEYOND BELIEF."
"HOW COULD WE MUSTER THE LEAST RESPECT FOR THESE AWKWARD SCRABBLERS-IN-THE-DIRT?"
"WE TORMENTED MAN WITH FOOLISH TRICKS. WE MADE HIM SUPERSTITIOUS AND FEARFUL. WE TOYED WITH HIS PRIDE."
BUT WE WERE NOT CONTENT TO END IT THERE.
CONFIDENT IN OUR SUPERIORITY, WE ALLOWED OURSELVES TO BECOME CRUEL.
"WE STOLE THE ESSENCE FROM HIS MILK AND CHEESE AND LEFT ONLY THE APPEARANCES BEHIND... AND THE MORE HE ATE, THE MORE HE STARVED."
"WE BEWITCHED HIS ANIMALS."
"WE BLIGHTED HIS CROPS."

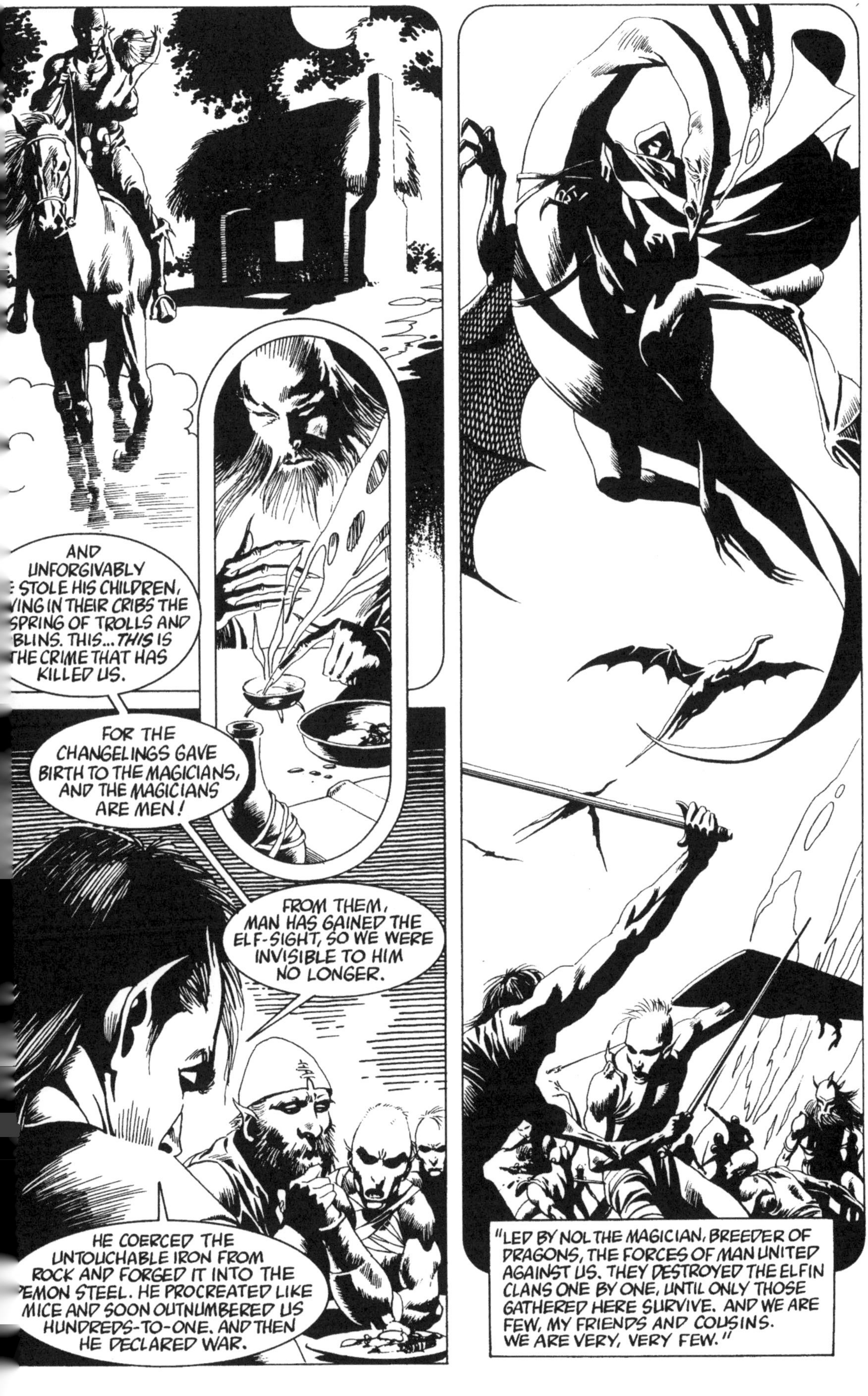

AND UNFORGIVABLY
E STOLE HIS CHILDREN,
VING IN THEIR CRIBS THE
SPRING OF TROLLS AND
BLINS. THIS... *THIS* IS
THE CRIME THAT HAS KILLED US.
FOR THE CHANGELINGS GAVE BIRTH TO THE MAGICIANS, AND THE MAGICIANS ARE MEN!
FROM THEM, MAN HAS GAINED THE ELF-SIGHT, SO WE WERE INVISIBLE TO HIM NO LONGER.
HE COERCED THE UNTOUCHABLE IRON FROM ROCK AND FORGED IT INTO THE
EMON STEEL. HE PROCREATED LIKE MICE AND SOON OUTNUMBERED US HUNDREDS-TO-ONE. AND THEN HE DECLARED WAR.
"LED BY NOL THE MAGICIAN, BREEDER OF DRAGONS, THE FORCES OF MAN UNITED AGAINST US. THEY DESTROYED THE ELFIN CLANS ONE BY ONE, UNTIL ONLY THOSE GATHERED HERE SURVIVE. AND WE ARE FEW, MY FRIENDS AND COUSINS. WE ARE VERY, VERY FEW."

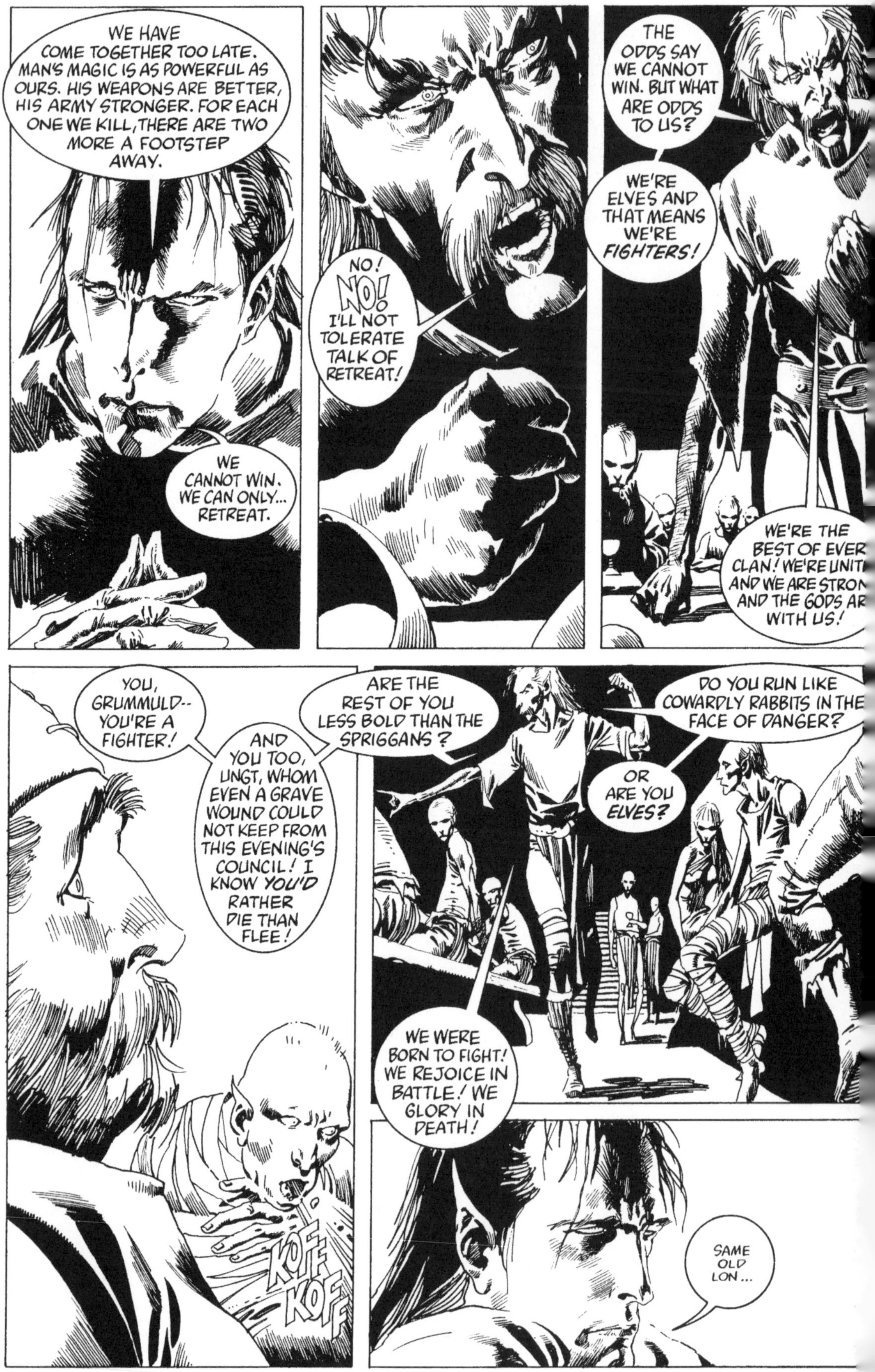
WE HAVE COME TOGETHER TOO LATE. MAN'S MAGIC IS AS POWERFUL AS OURS. HIS WEAPONS ARE BETTER, HIS ARMY STRONGER. FOR EACH ONE WE KILL, THERE ARE TWO MORE A FOOTSTEP AWAY.
WE CANNOT WIN. WE CAN ONLY... RETREAT.
NO! NO! I'LL NOT TOLERATE TALK OF RETREAT!
THE ODDS SAY WE CANNOT WIN. BUT WHAT ARE ODDS TO US?
WE'RE ELVES AND THAT MEANS WE'RE FIGHTERS!
WE'RE THE BEST OF EVER CLAN! WE'RE UNIT AND WE ARE STRON AND THE GODS AR WITH US!
YOU, GRUMMULD-- YOU'RE A FIGHTER!
AND YOU TOO, UNGT, WHOM EVEN A GRAVE WOUND COULD NOT KEEP FROM THIS EVENING'S COUNCIL! I KNOW YOU'D RATHER DIE THAN FLEE!
KOFF KOFF
ARE THE REST OF YOU LESS BOLD THAN THE SPRIGGANS?
DO YOU RUN LIKE COWARDLY RABBITS IN THE FACE OF DANGER?
OR ARE YOU ELVES?
WE WERE BORN TO FIGHT! WE REJOICE IN BATTLE! WE GLORY IN DEATH!
SAME OLD LON...

OR HOURS THE ARGUMENT RAGES, CALM REASON AGAINST HEATED EMOTION. TIROL PLEADS HIS CASE LOQUENTLY; LON MATCHES HIM POINT FOR POINT. THE ALE FLOWS AND PASSIONS RUN HIGH.

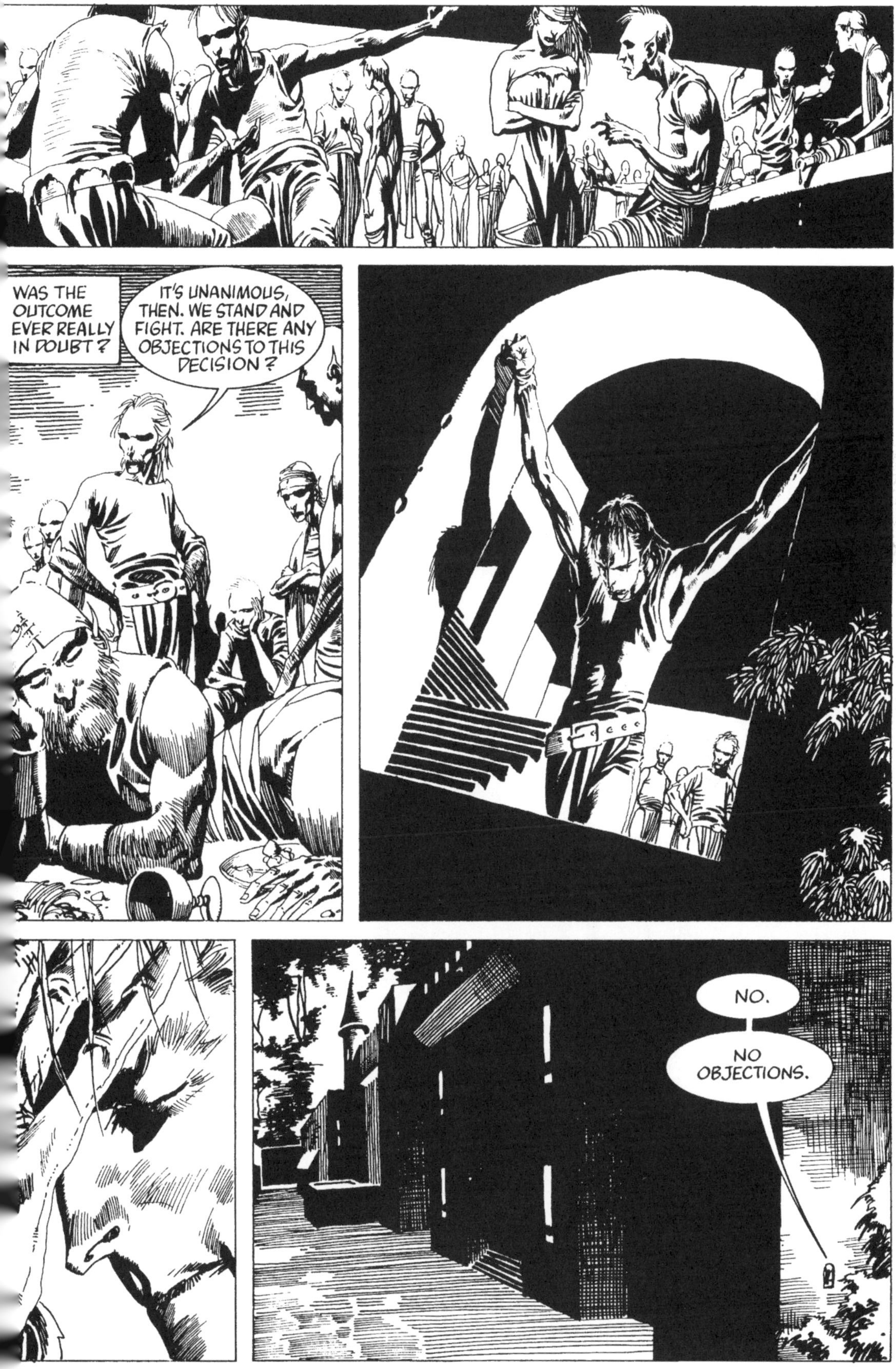

WAS THE OUTCOME EVER REALLY IN DOUBT?
IT'S UNANIMOUS, THEN. WE STAND AND FIGHT. ARE THERE ANY OBJECTIONS TO THIS DECISION?
NO.
NO OBJECTIONS.

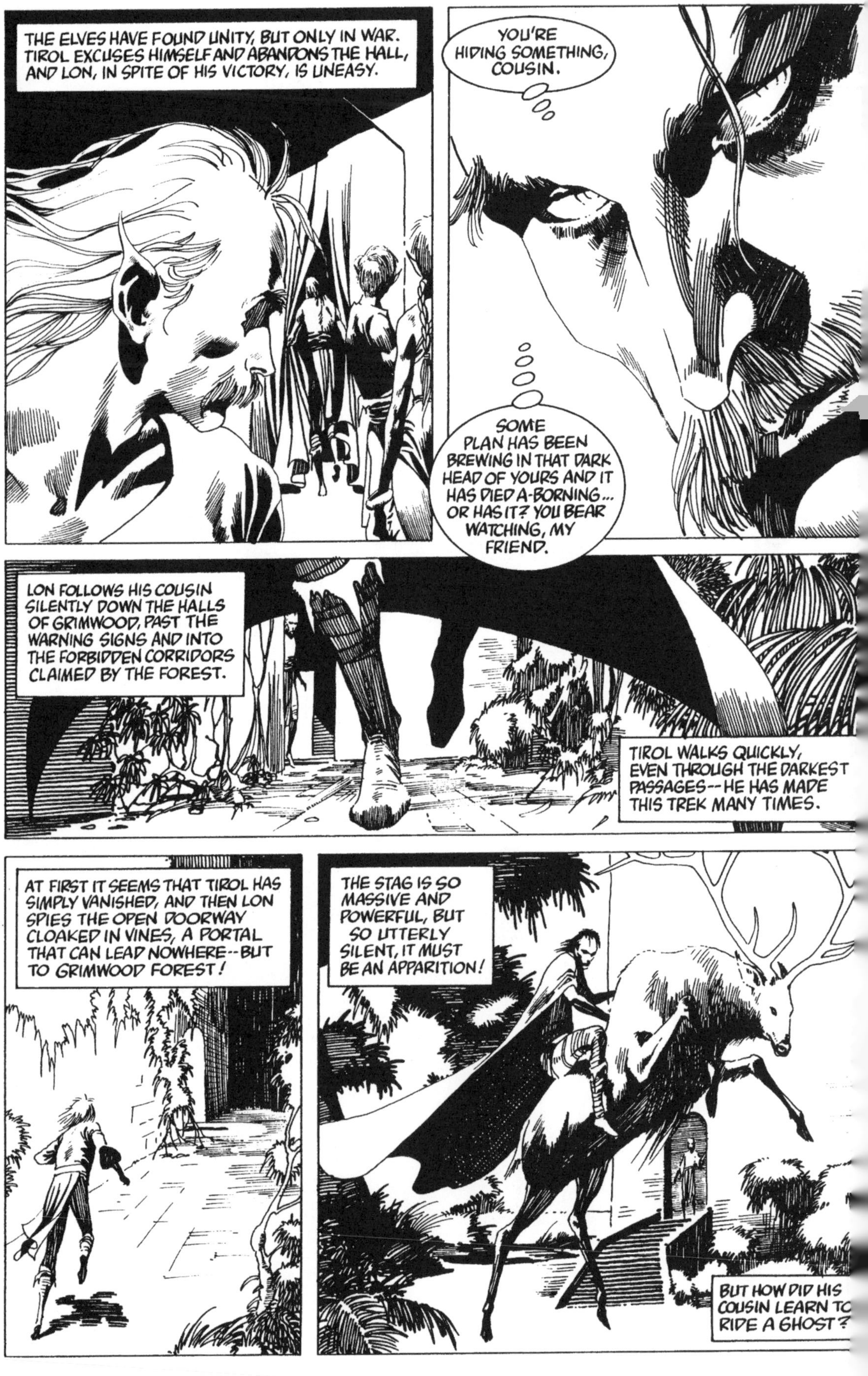
THE ELVES HAVE FOUND UNITY, BUT ONLY IN WAR. TIROL EXCUSES HIMSELF AND ABANDONS THE HALL, AND LON, IN SPITE OF HIS VICTORY, IS UNEASY.
YOU'RE HIDING SOMETHING, COUSIN.
SOME PLAN HAS BEEN BREWING IN THAT DARK HEAD OF YOURS AND IT HAS DIED A-BORNING... OR HAS IT? YOU BEAR WATCHING, MY FRIEND.
LON FOLLOWS HIS COUSIN SILENTLY DOWN THE HALLS OF GRIMWOOD, PAST THE WARNING SIGNS AND INTO THE FORBIDDEN CORRIDORS CLAIMED BY THE FOREST.
TIROL WALKS QUICKLY, EVEN THROUGH THE DARKEST PASSAGES--HE HAS MADE THIS TREK MANY TIMES.
AT FIRST IT SEEMS THAT TIROL HAS SIMPLY VANISHED, AND THEN LON SPIES THE OPEN DOORWAY CLOAKED IN VINES, A PORTAL THAT CAN LEAD NOWHERE--BUT TO GRIMWOOD FOREST!
THE STAG IS SO MASSIVE AND POWERFUL, BUT SO UTTERLY SILENT, IT MUST BE AN APPARITION!
BUT HOW DID HIS COUSIN LEARN TO RIDE A GHOST?

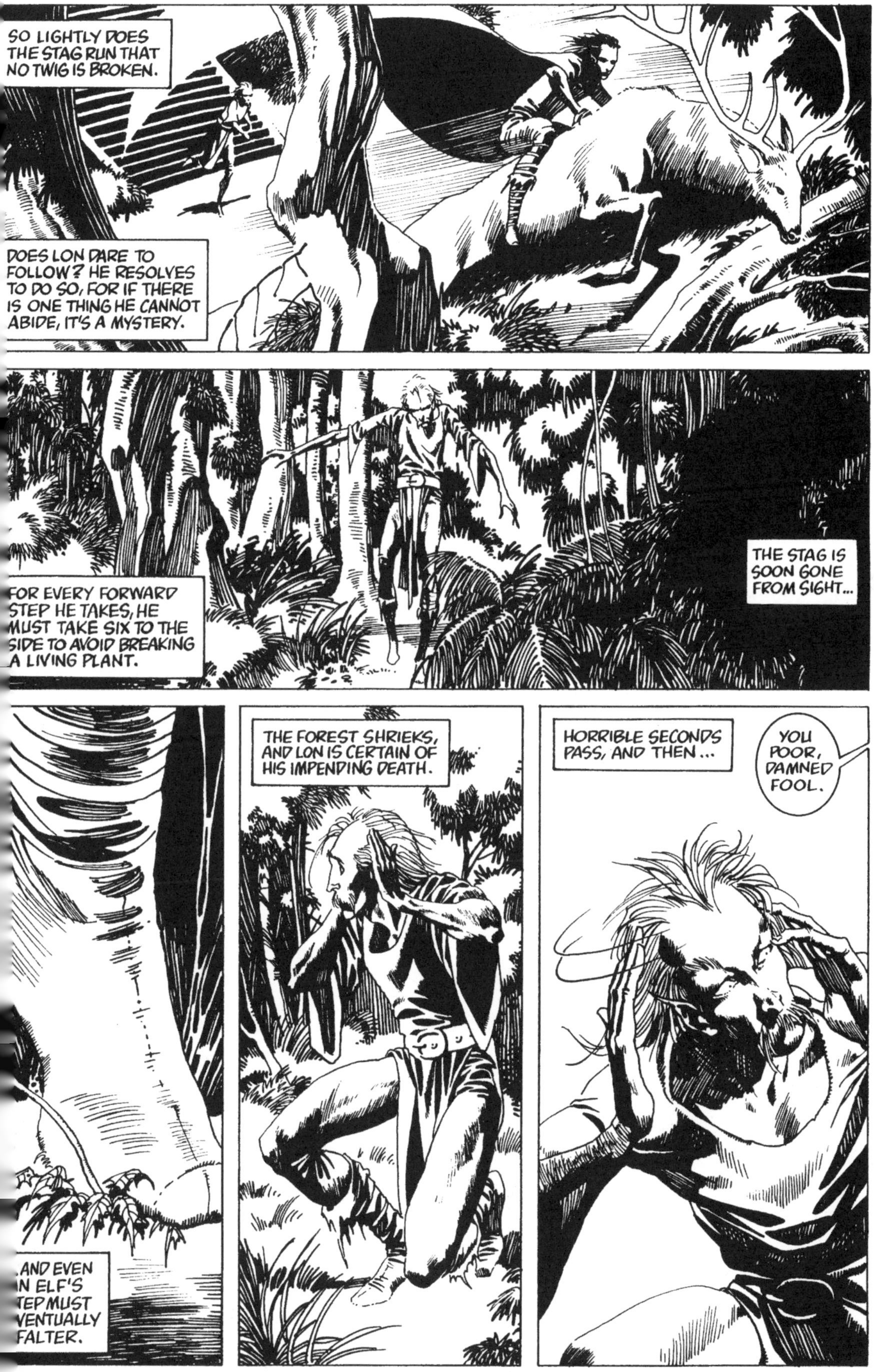
SO LIGHTLY DOES THE STAG RUN THAT NO TWIG IS BROKEN.
DOES LON DARE TO FOLLOW? HE RESOLVES TO DO SO, FOR IF THERE IS ONE THING HE CANNOT ABIDE, IT'S A MYSTERY.
FOR EVERY FORWARD STEP HE TAKES, HE MUST TAKE SIX TO THE SIDE TO AVOID BREAKING A LIVING PLANT.
THE STAG IS SOON GONE FROM SIGHT...
.AND EVEN N ELF'S TEP MUST VENTUALLY FALTER.
THE FOREST SHRIEKS, AND LON IS CERTAIN OF HIS IMPENDING DEATH.
HORRIBLE SECONDS PASS, AND THEN...
YOU POOR, DAMNED FOOL.

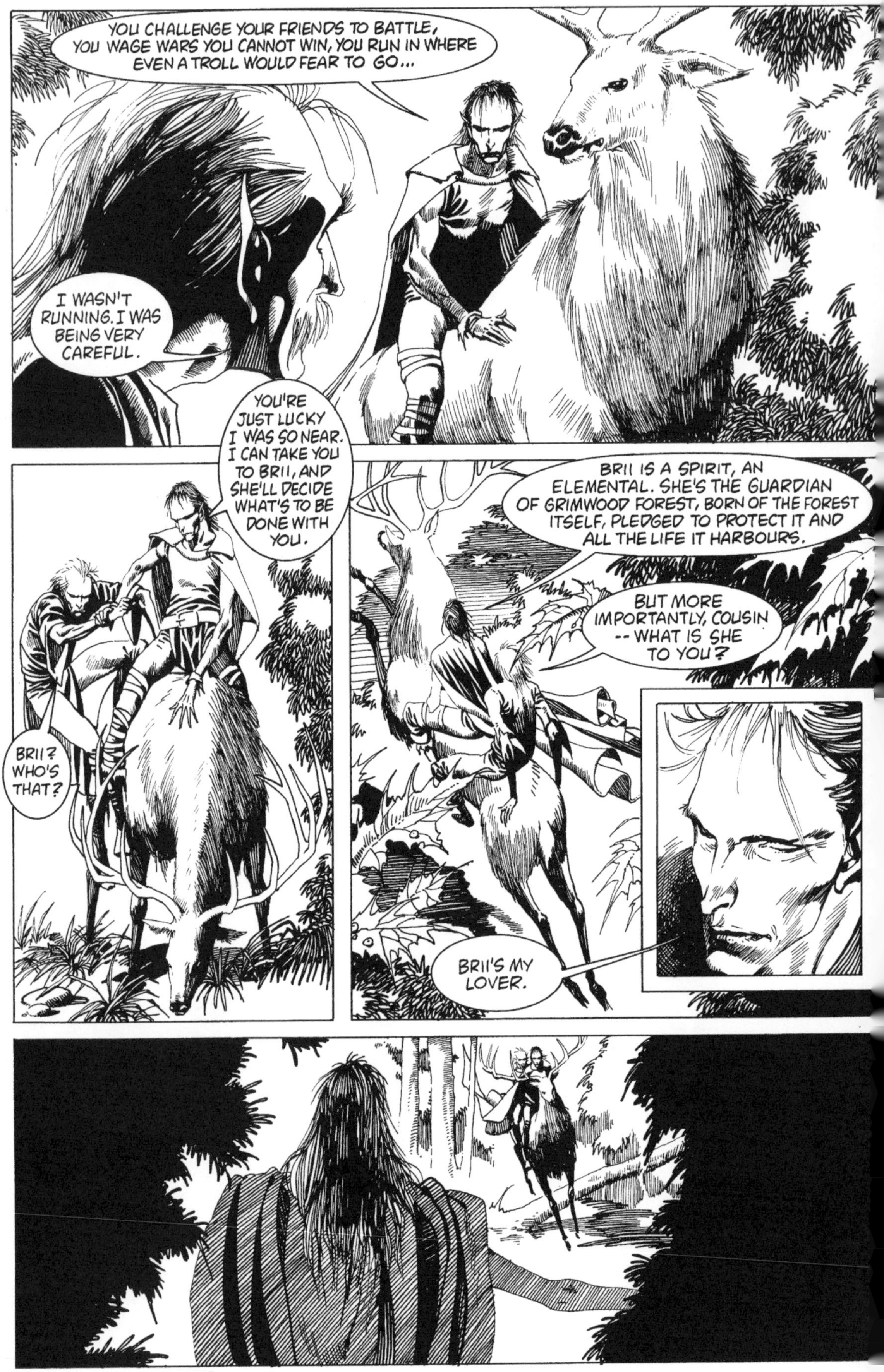

YOU CHALLENGE YOUR FRIENDS TO BATTLE, YOU WAGE WARS YOU CANNOT WIN, YOU RUN IN WHERE EVEN A TROLL WOULD FEAR TO GO...
I WASN'T RUNNING. I WAS BEING VERY CAREFUL.
YOU'RE JUST LUCKY I WAS SO NEAR. I CAN TAKE YOU TO BRII, AND SHE'LL DECIDE WHAT'S TO BE DONE WITH YOU.
BRII? WHO'S THAT?
BRII IS A SPIRIT, AN ELEMENTAL. SHE'S THE GUARDIAN OF GRIMWOOD FOREST, BORN OF THE FOREST ITSELF, PLEDGED TO PROTECT IT AND ALL THE LIFE IT HARBOURS.
BUT MORE IMPORTANTLY, COUSIN -- WHAT IS SHE TO YOU?
BRII'S MY LOVER.

GRIMWOOD'S DAUGHTER

H A P T E R   T H R E E

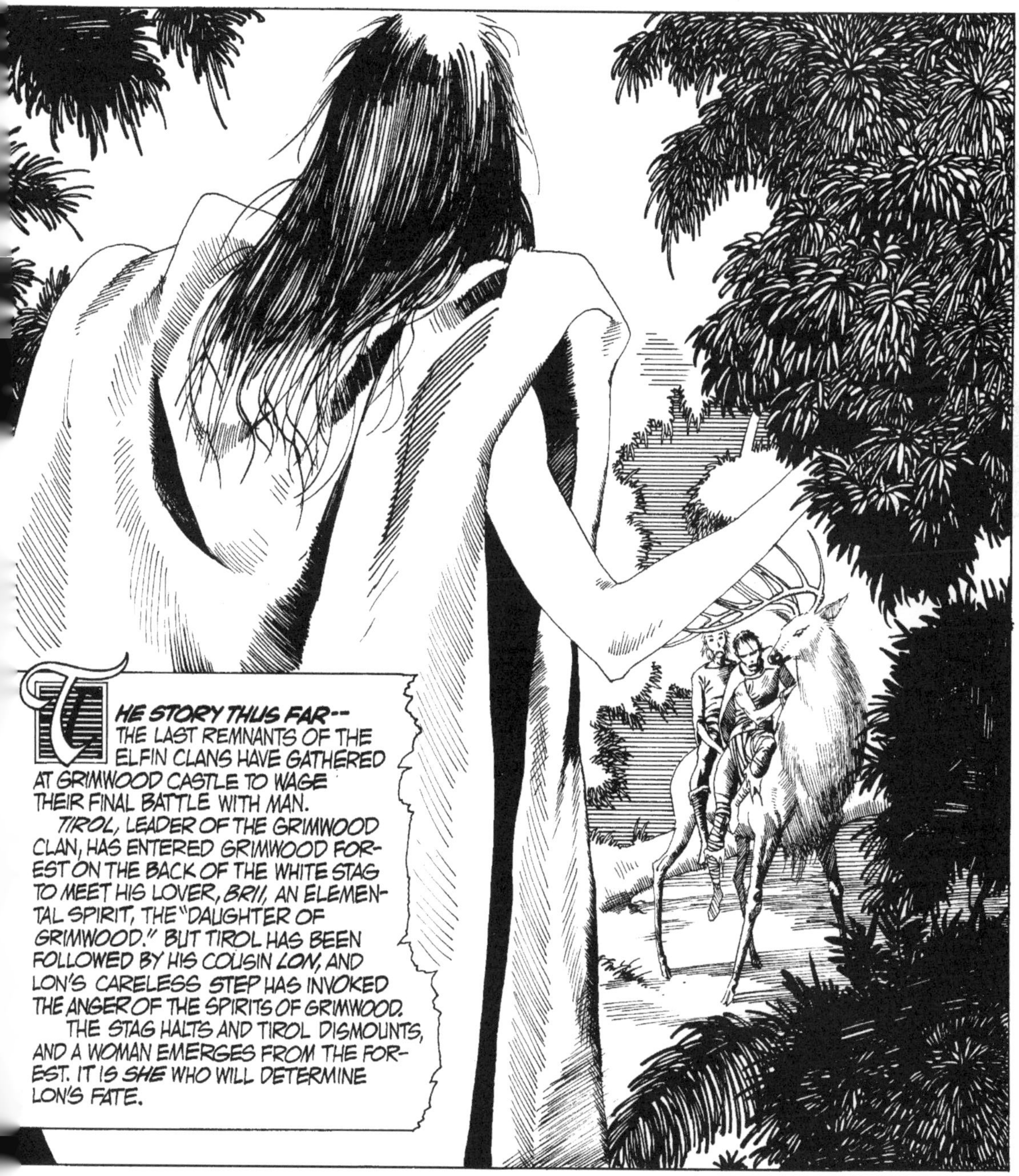
THE STORY THUS FAR-- THE LAST REMNANTS OF THE ELFIN CLANS HAVE GATHERED AT GRIMWOOD CASTLE TO WAGE THEIR FINAL BATTLE WITH MAN.
TIROL, LEADER OF THE GRIMWOOD CLAN, HAS ENTERED GRIMWOOD FOREST ON THE BACK OF THE WHITE STAG TO MEET HIS LOVER, BRII, AN ELEMENTAL SPIRIT, THE "DAUGHTER OF GRIMWOOD." BUT TIROL HAS BEEN FOLLOWED BY HIS COUSIN LON, AND LON'S CARELESS STEP HAS INVOKED THE ANGER OF THE SPIRITS OF GRIMWOOD.
THE STAG HALTS AND TIROL DISMOUNTS, AND A WOMAN EMERGES FROM THE FOREST. IT IS SHE WHO WILL DETERMINE LON'S FATE.

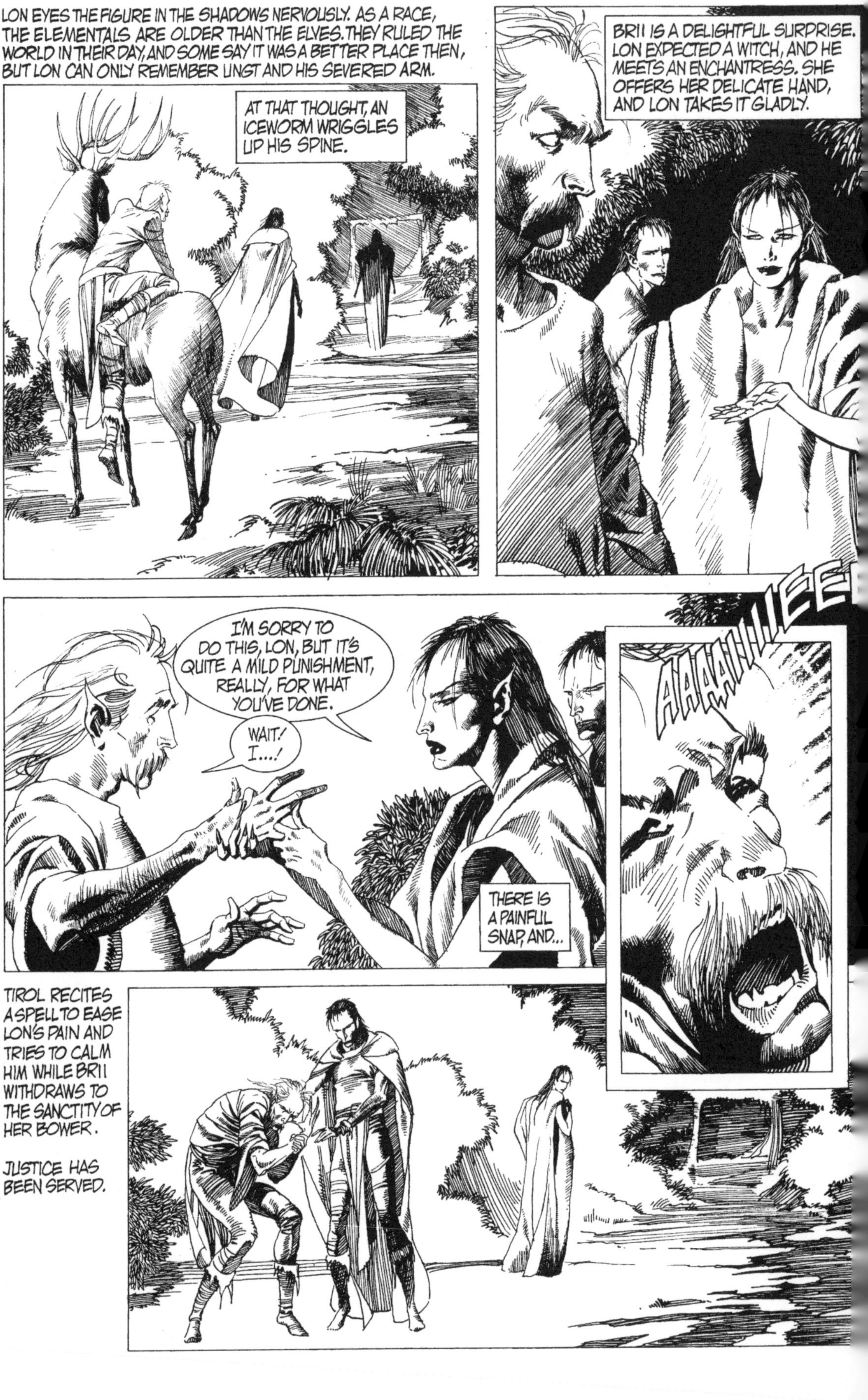
LON EYES THE FIGURE IN THE SHADOWS NERVOUSLY. AS A RACE, THE ELEMENTALS ARE OLDER THAN THE ELVES. THEY RULED THE WORLD IN THEIR DAY, AND SOME SAY IT WAS A BETTER PLACE THEN, BUT LON CAN ONLY REMEMBER UNGT AND HIS SEVERED ARM.
AT THAT THOUGHT, AN ICEWORM WRIGGLES UP HIS SPINE.
BRII IS A DELIGHTFUL SURPRISE. LON EXPECTED A WITCH, AND HE MEETS AN ENCHANTRESS. SHE OFFERS HER DELICATE HAND, AND LON TAKES IT GLADLY.
I'M SORRY TO DO THIS, LON, BUT IT'S QUITE A MILD PUNISHMENT, REALLY, FOR WHAT YOU'VE DONE.
WAIT! I...!
THERE IS A PAINFUL SNAP, AND...
AAAAHIIEEE
TIROL RECITES A SPELL TO EASE LON'S PAIN AND TRIES TO CALM HIM WHILE BRII WITHDRAWS TO THE SANCTITY OF HER BOWER.
JUSTICE HAS BEEN SERVED.

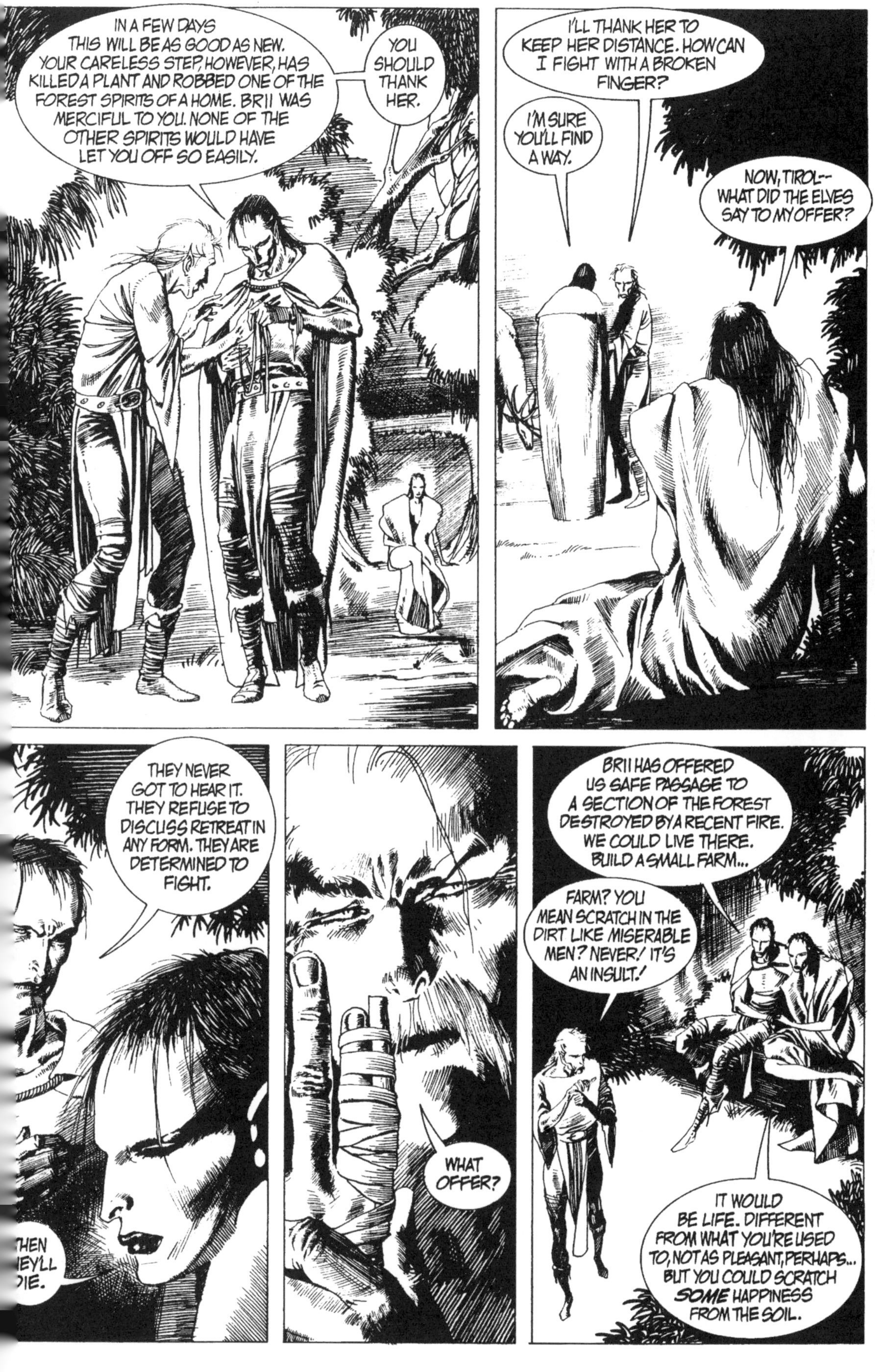
IN A FEW DAYS THIS WILL BE AS GOOD AS NEW. YOUR CARELESS STEP, HOWEVER, HAS KILLED A PLANT AND ROBBED ONE OF THE FOREST SPIRITS OF A HOME. BRII WAS MERCIFUL TO YOU. NONE OF THE OTHER SPIRITS WOULD HAVE LET YOU OFF SO EASILY.
YOU SHOULD THANK HER.
I'LL THANK HER TO KEEP HER DISTANCE. HOW CAN I FIGHT WITH A BROKEN FINGER?
I'M SURE YOU'LL FIND A WAY.
NOW, TIROL-- WHAT DID THE ELVES SAY TO MY OFFER?
THEY NEVER GOT TO HEAR IT. THEY REFUSE TO DISCUSS RETREAT IN ANY FORM. THEY ARE DETERMINED TO FIGHT.
THEN EY'LL IE.
WHAT OFFER?
BRII HAS OFFERED US SAFE PASSAGE TO A SECTION OF THE FOREST DESTROYED BY A RECENT FIRE. WE COULD LIVE THERE. BUILD A SMALL FARM...
FARM? YOU MEAN SCRATCH IN THE DIRT LIKE MISERABLE MEN? NEVER! IT'S AN INSULT!
IT WOULD BE LIFE. DIFFERENT FROM WHAT YOU'RE USED TO, NOT AS PLEASANT, PERHAPS... BUT YOU COULD SCRATCH SOME HAPPINESS FROM THE SOIL.

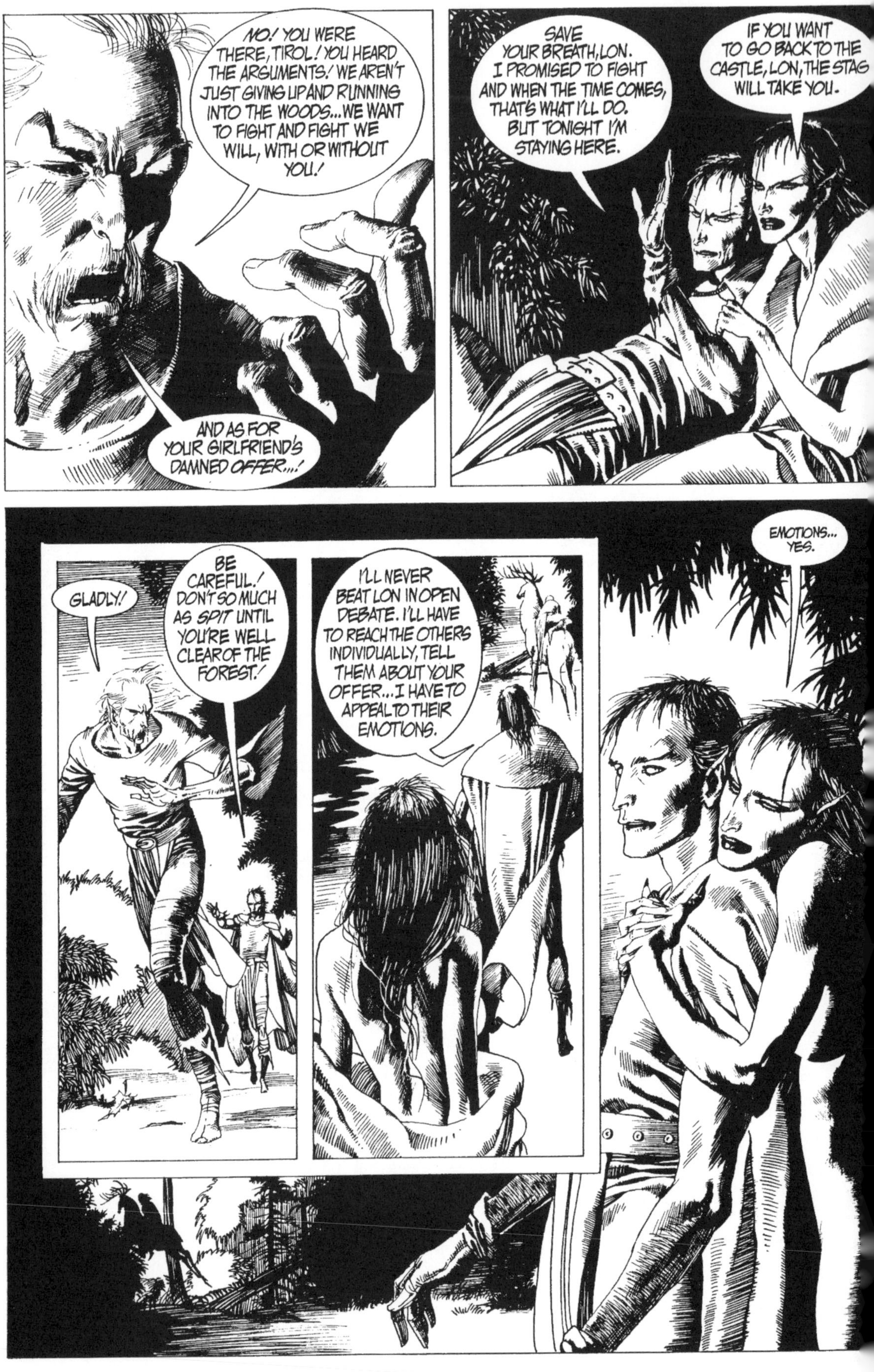
NO! YOU WERE THERE, TIROL! YOU HEARD THE ARGUMENTS! WE AREN'T JUST GIVING UP AND RUNNING INTO THE WOODS...WE WANT TO FIGHT AND FIGHT WE WILL, WITH OR WITHOUT YOU!
AND AS FOR YOUR GIRLFRIEND'S DAMNED OFFER...!
SAVE YOUR BREATH, LON. I PROMISED TO FIGHT AND WHEN THE TIME COMES, THAT'S WHAT I'LL DO. BUT TONIGHT I'M STAYING HERE.
IF YOU WANT TO GO BACK TO THE CASTLE, LON, THE STAG WILL TAKE YOU.
GLADLY!
BE CAREFUL! DON'T SO MUCH AS SPIT UNTIL YOU'RE WELL CLEAR OF THE FOREST!
I'LL NEVER BEAT LON IN OPEN DEBATE. I'LL HAVE TO REACH THE OTHERS INDIVIDUALLY, TELL THEM ABOUT YOUR OFFER...I HAVE TO APPEAL TO THEIR EMOTIONS.
EMOTIONS... YES.

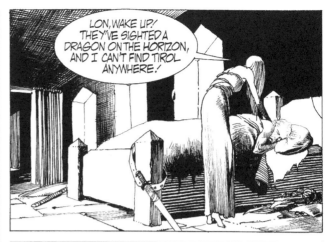

LON, WAKE UP! THEY'VE SIGHTED A DRAGON ON THE HORIZON, AND I CAN'T FIND TIROL ANYWHERE!

TIROL IS... OUT. JUST ONE DRAGON?

SO FAR, BUT THEY'RE CALLING FOR TIROL ON THE BATTLEMENTS!

IT'S ONE OF NOL'S ALL RIGHT-- MAYBE THE OLD DRAGON-BREEDER HIMSELF! FLYING TOO HIGH FOR US TO DO HIM ANY HARM.

WHERE'S THAT DAMN TIROL?

SOUND THE WAR HORN! WE HAVE TO CALL TIROL BACK BEFORE THEY ATTACK!

WE'LL KNOW IN A MINUTE. SOUND THAT HORN!

YOU THINK IT'S THE MERCY RUN, THEN?

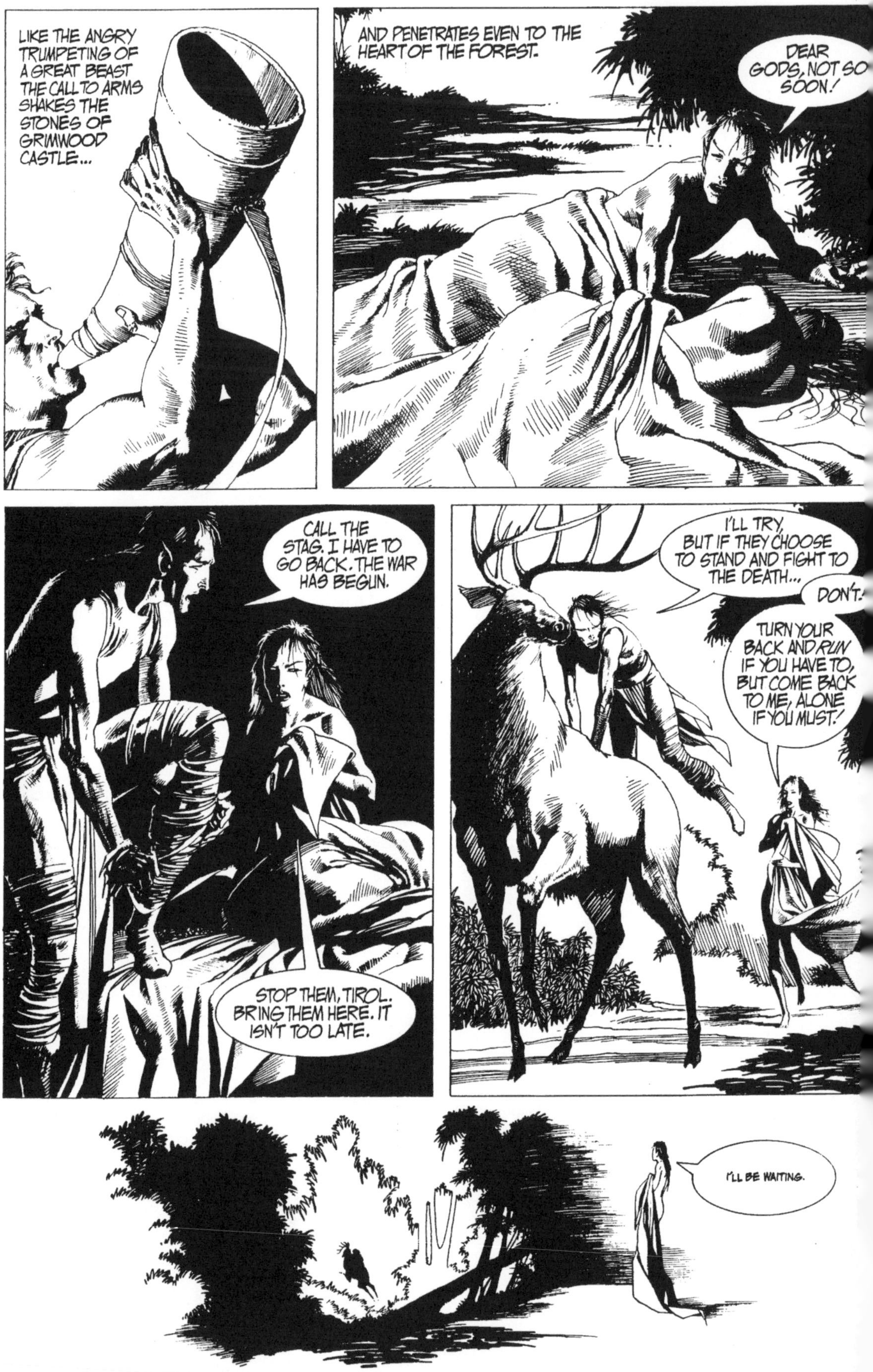
LIKE THE ANGRY TRUMPETING OF A GREAT BEAST THE CALL TO ARMS SHAKES THE STONES OF GRIMWOOD CASTLE...
AND PENETRATES EVEN TO THE HEART OF THE FOREST.
DEAR GODS, NOT SO SOON!
CALL THE STAG. I HAVE TO GO BACK. THE WAR HAS BEGUN.
STOP THEM, TIROL. BRING THEM HERE. IT ISN'T TOO LATE.
I'LL TRY, BUT IF THEY CHOOSE TO STAND AND FIGHT TO THE DEATH...
DON'T.
TURN YOUR BACK AND RUN IF YOU HAVE TO, BUT COME BACK TO ME, ALONE IF YOU MUST!
I'LL BE WAITING.

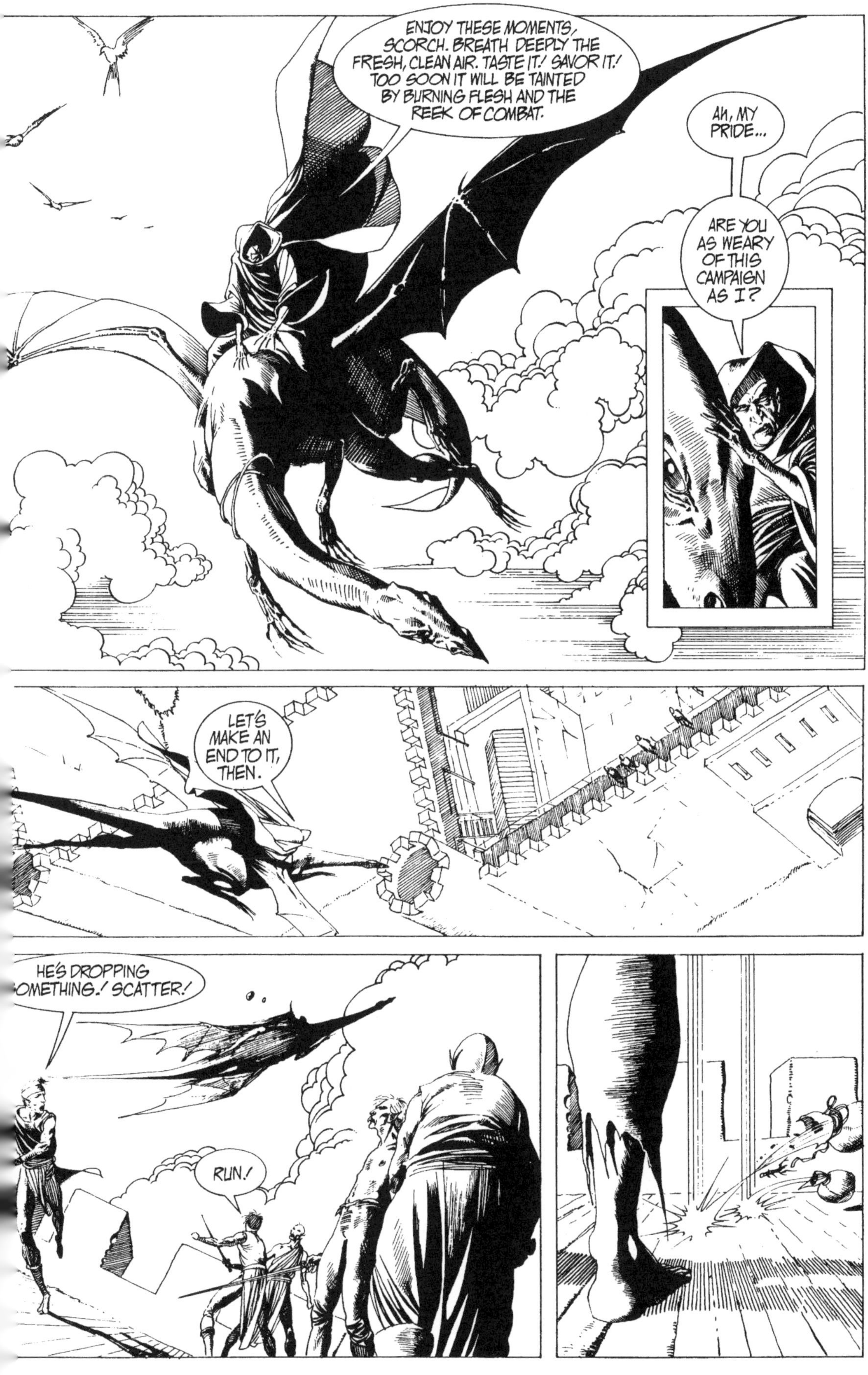
ENJOY THESE MOMENTS, SCORCH. BREATH DEEPLY THE FRESH, CLEAN AIR. TASTE IT! SAVOR IT! TOO SOON IT WILL BE TAINTED BY BURNING FLESH AND THE REEK OF COMBAT.
AH, MY PRIDE...
ARE YOU AS WEARY OF THIS CAMPAIGN AS I?
LET'S MAKE AN END TO IT, THEN.
HE'S DROPPING SOMETHING! SCATTER!
RUN!

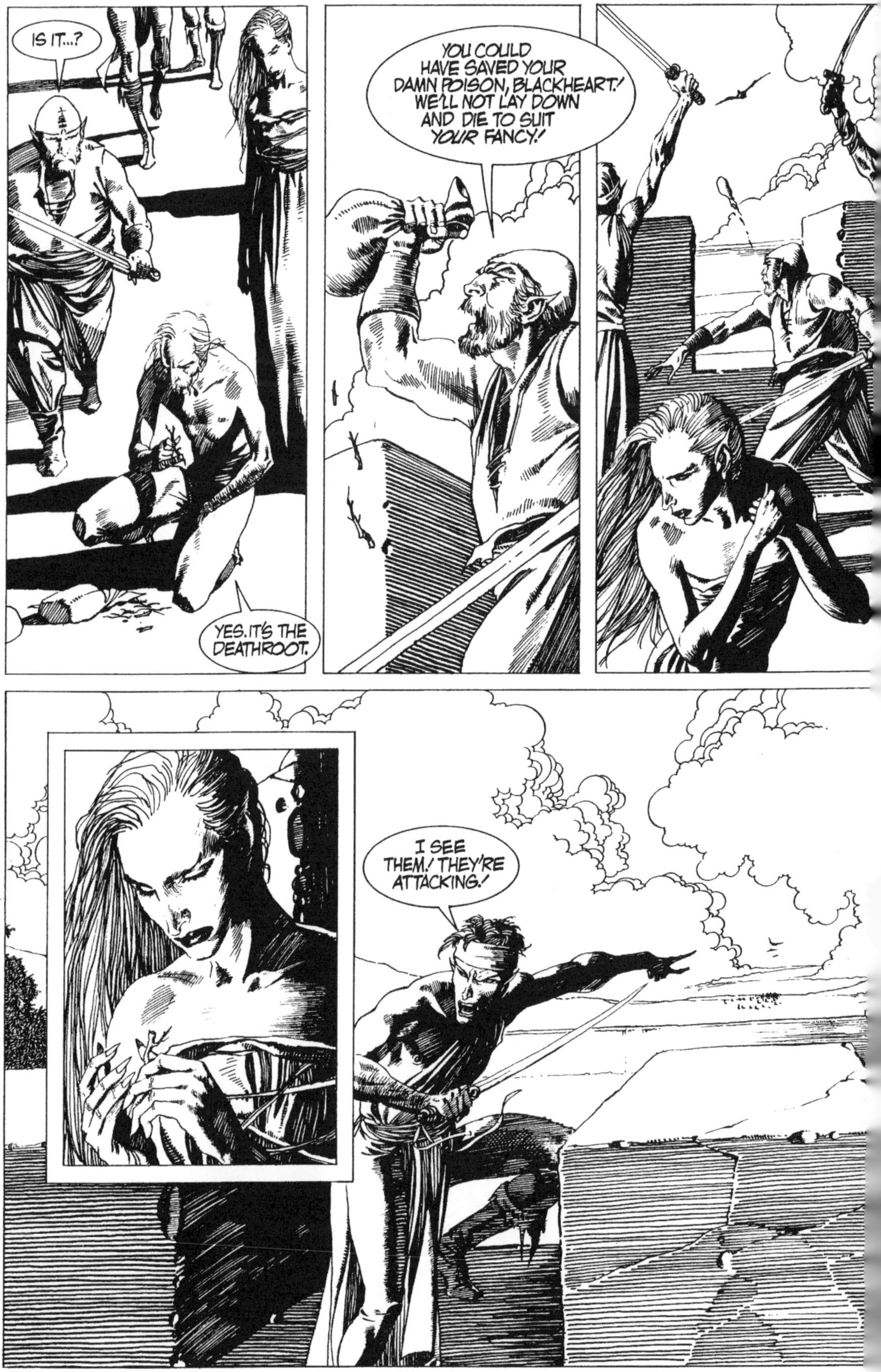
IS IT...?
YES. IT'S THE DEATHROOT.
YOU COULD HAVE SAVED YOUR DAMN POISON, BLACKHEART! WE'LL NOT LAY DOWN AND DIE TO SUIT YOUR FANCY!
I SEE THEM! THEY'RE ATTACKING!

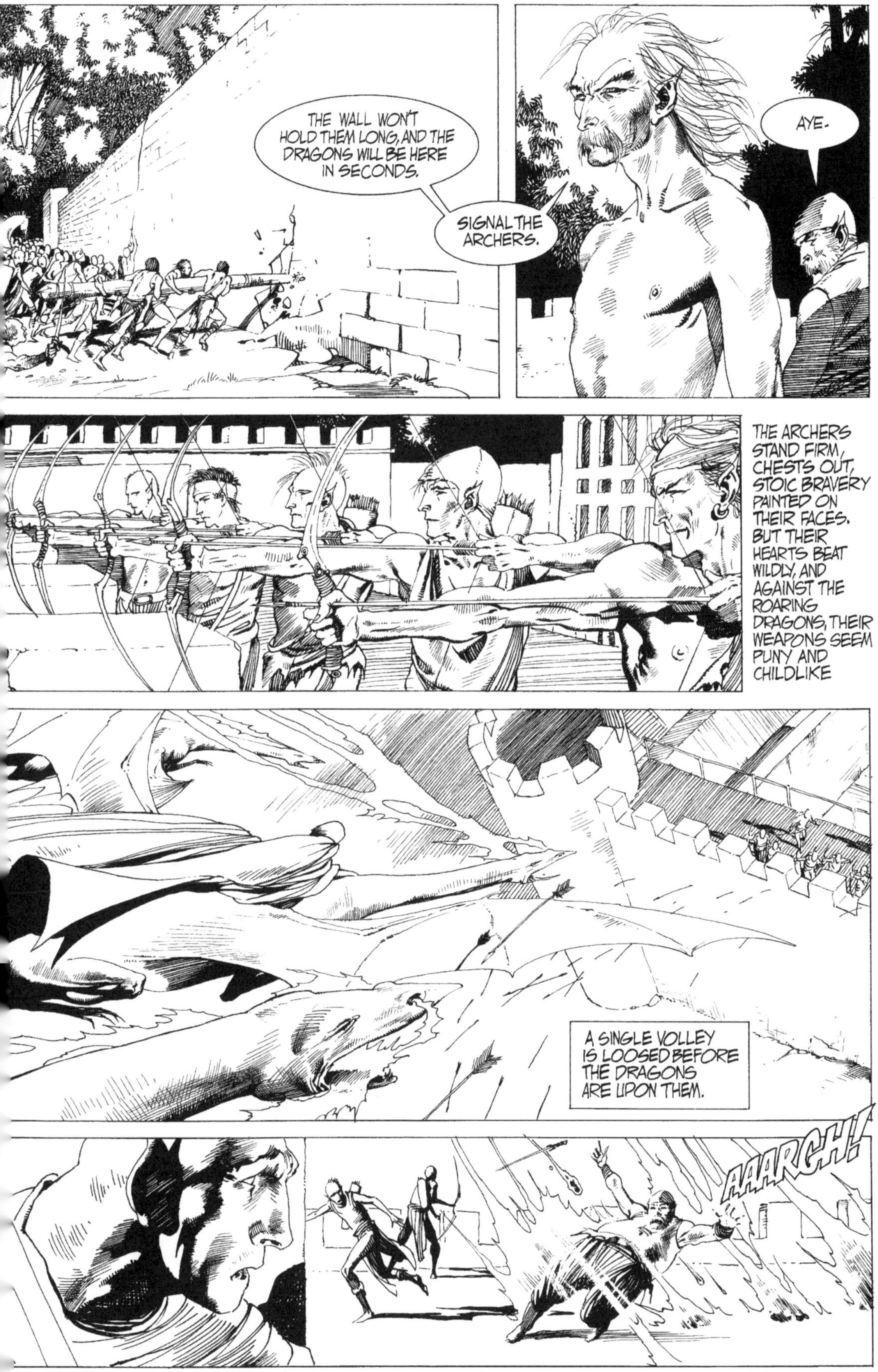
THE WALL WON'T HOLD THEM LONG, AND THE DRAGONS WILL BE HERE IN SECONDS.
SIGNAL THE ARCHERS.
AYE.
THE ARCHERS STAND FIRM, CHESTS OUT, STOIC BRAVERY PAINTED ON THEIR FACES. BUT THEIR HEARTS BEAT WILDLY, AND AGAINST THE ROARING DRAGONS, THEIR WEAPONS SEEM PUNY AND CHILDLIKE
A SINGLE VOLLEY IS LOOSED BEFORE THE DRAGONS ARE UPON THEM.
AAARGH!

GRIMWOOD'S DAUGHTER

CHAPTER FOU

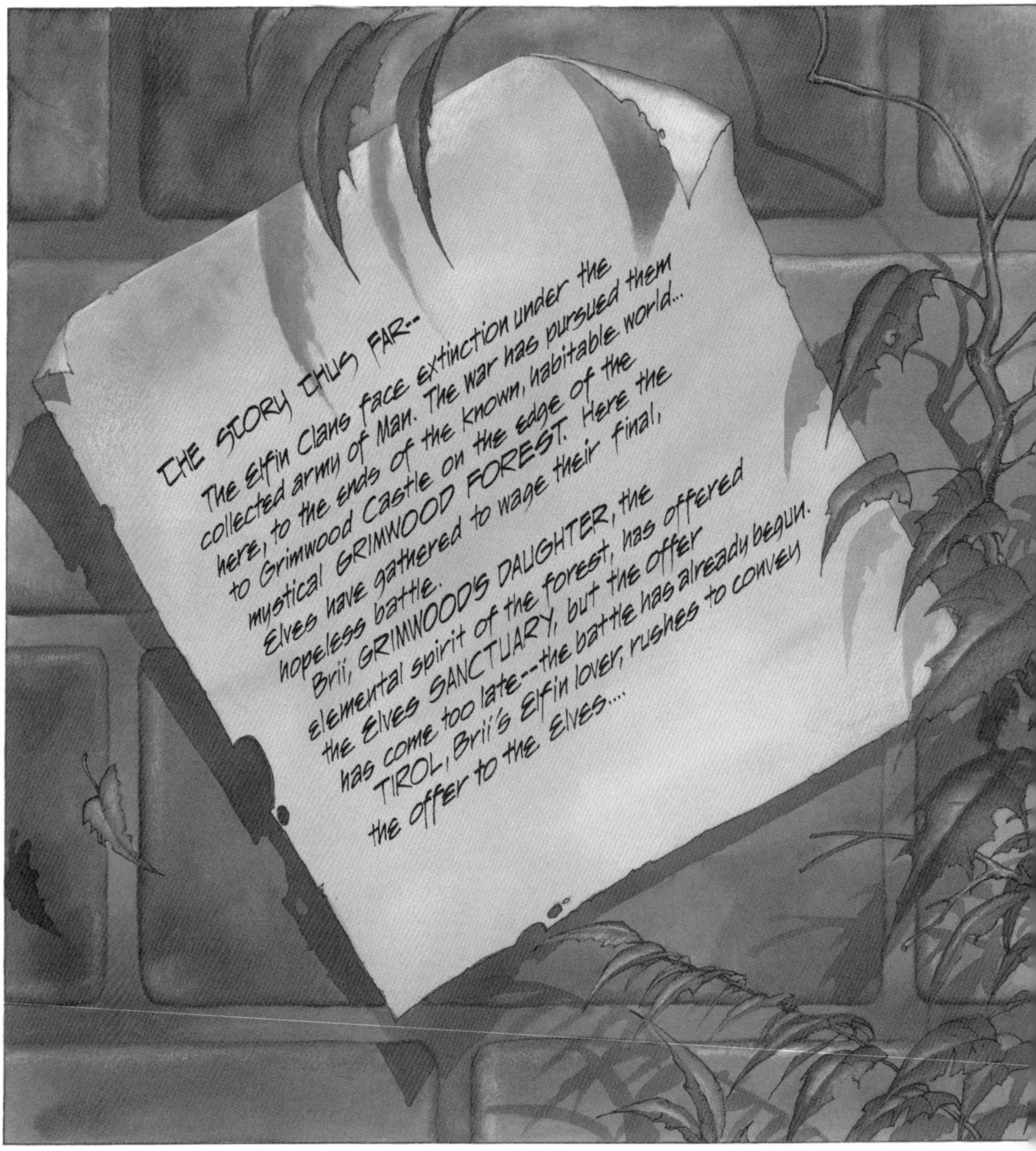
THE STORY THUS FAR--
The Elfin Clans face extinction under the collected army of Man. The war has pursued them here, to the ends of the known, habitable world... to Grimwood Castle on the edge of the mystical GRIMWOOD FOREST. Here the Elves have gathered to wage their final, hopeless battle.
Brii, GRIMWOOD'S DAUGHTER, the elemental spirit of the forest, has offered the Elves SANCTUARY, but the offer has come too late--the battle has already begun. TIROL, Brii's Elfin lover, rushes to convey the offer to the Elves....

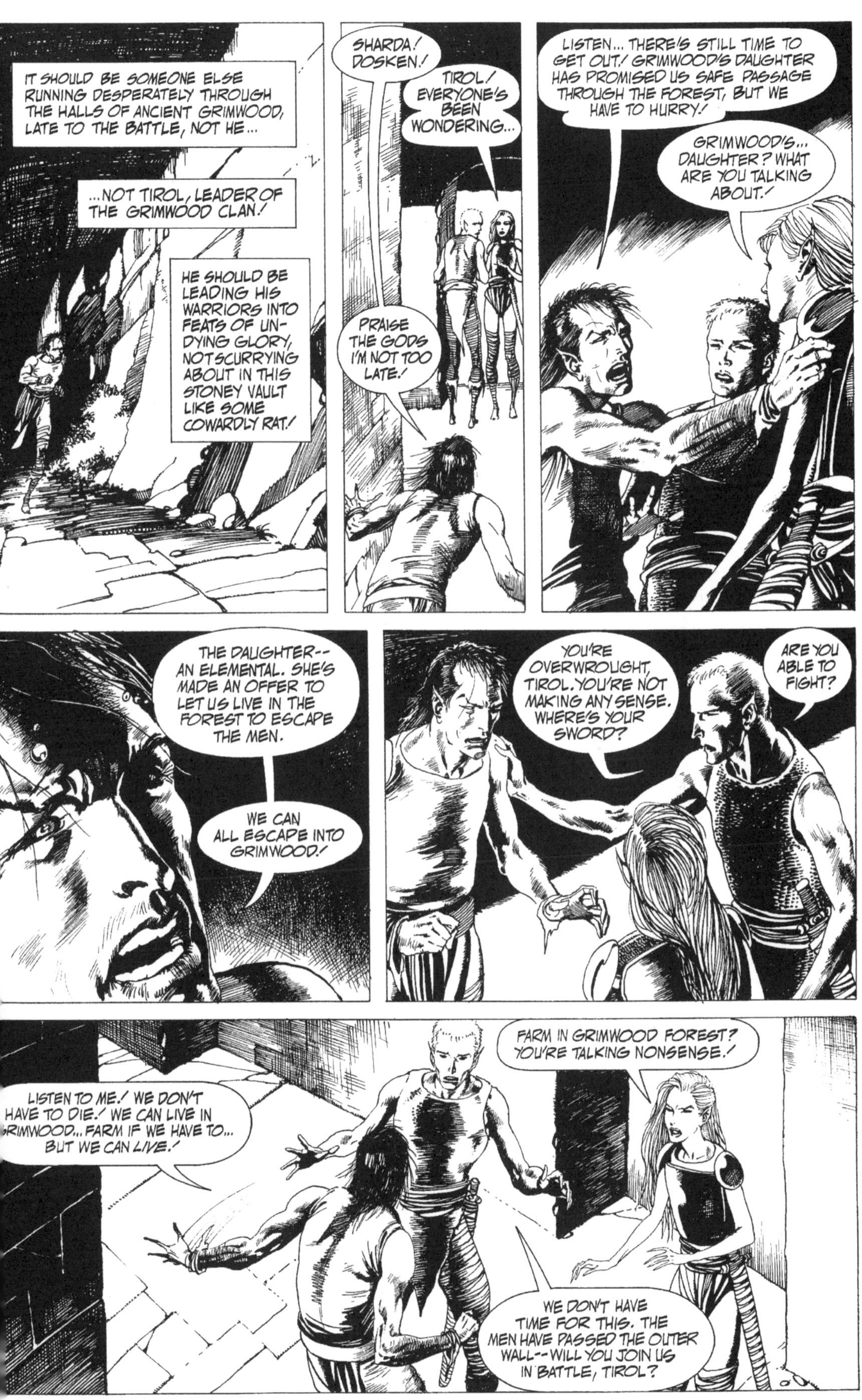
IT SHOULD BE SOMEONE ELSE RUNNING DESPERATELY THROUGH THE HALLS OF ANCIENT GRIMWOOD, LATE TO THE BATTLE, NOT HE...
...NOT TIROL, LEADER OF THE GRIMWOOD CLAN!
HE SHOULD BE LEADING HIS WARRIORS INTO FEATS OF UN-DYING GLORY, NOT SCURRYING ABOUT IN THIS STONEY VAULT LIKE SOME COWARDLY RAT!
SHARDA! DOSKEN!
TIROL! EVERYONE'S BEEN WONDERING...
PRAISE THE GODS I'M NOT TOO LATE!
LISTEN... THERE'S STILL TIME TO GET OUT! GRIMWOOD'S DAUGHTER HAS PROMISED US SAFE PASSAGE THROUGH THE FOREST, BUT WE HAVE TO HURRY!
GRIMWOOD'S... DAUGHTER? WHAT ARE YOU TALKING ABOUT!
THE DAUGHTER-- AN ELEMENTAL. SHE'S MADE AN OFFER TO LET US LIVE IN THE FOREST TO ESCAPE THE MEN.
WE CAN ALL ESCAPE INTO GRIMWOOD!
YOU'RE OVERWROUGHT, TIROL. YOU'RE NOT MAKING ANY SENSE. WHERE'S YOUR SWORD?
ARE YOU ABLE TO FIGHT?
LISTEN TO ME! WE DON'T HAVE TO DIE! WE CAN LIVE IN GRIMWOOD... FARM IF WE HAVE TO... BUT WE CAN LIVE!
FARM IN GRIMWOOD FOREST? YOU'RE TALKING NONSENSE!
WE DON'T HAVE TIME FOR THIS. THE MEN HAVE PASSED THE OUTER WALL-- WILL YOU JOIN US IN BATTLE, TIROL?

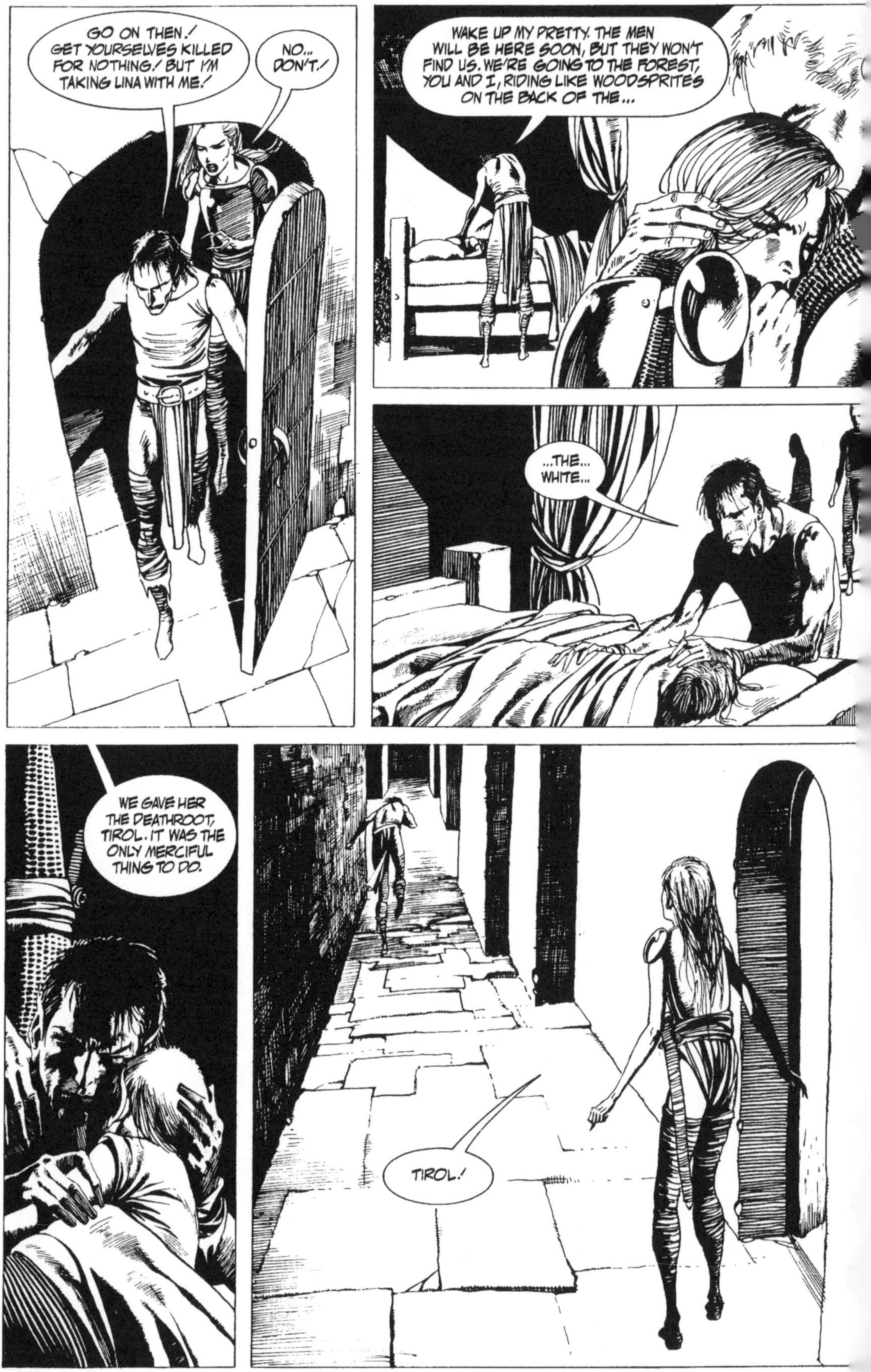
GO ON THEN.! GET YOURSELVES KILLED FOR NOTHING.! BUT I'M TAKING LINA WITH ME.!
NO... DON'T.!
WAKE UP MY PRETTY. THE MEN WILL BE HERE SOON, BUT THEY WON'T FIND US. WE'RE GOING TO THE FOREST, YOU AND I, RIDING LIKE WOODSPRITES ON THE BACK OF THE...
...THE... WHITE...
WE GAVE HER THE DEATHROOT, TIROL. IT WAS THE ONLY MERCIFUL THING TO DO.
TIROL.!

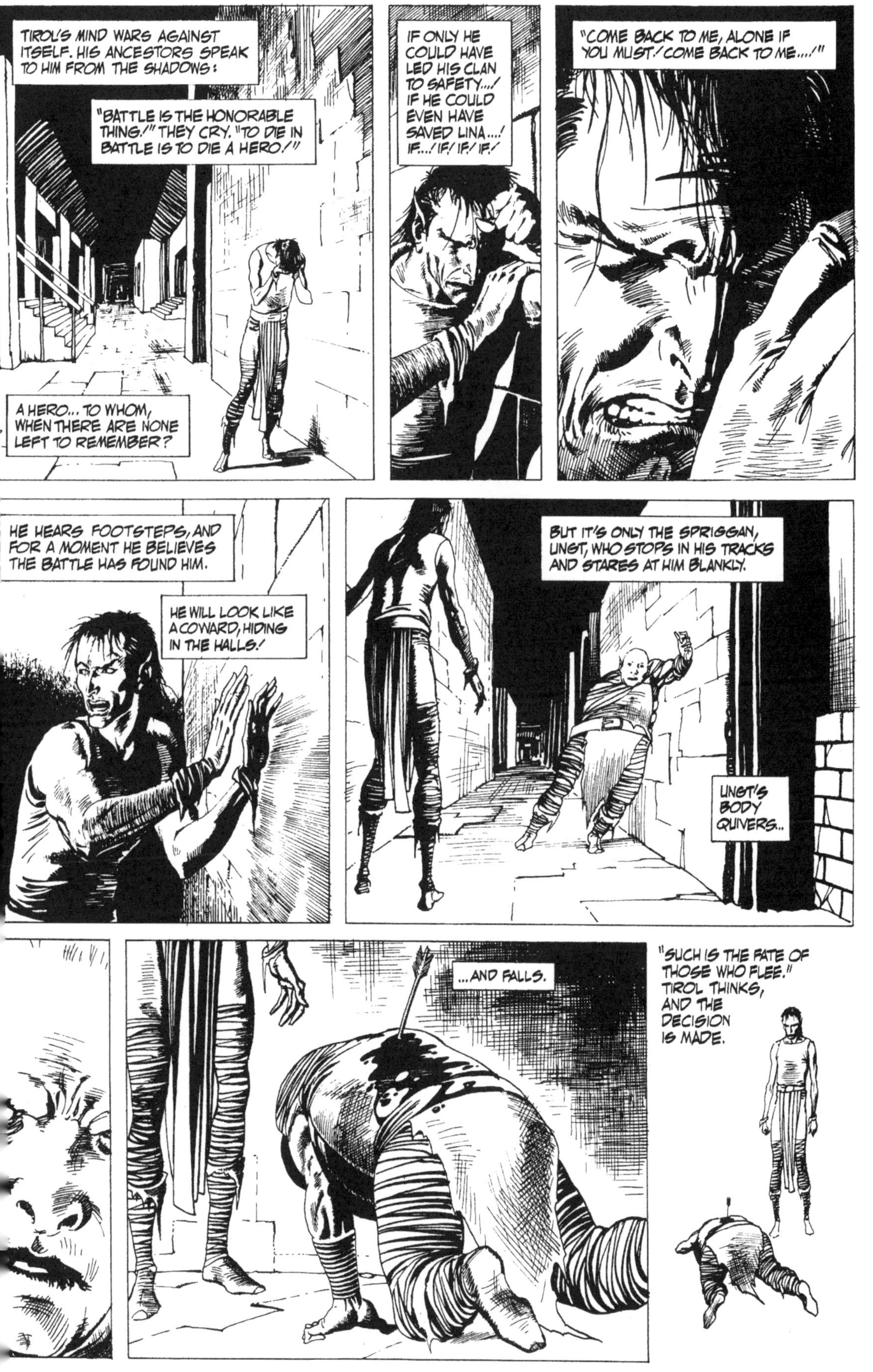
TIROL'S MIND WARS AGAINST ITSELF. HIS ANCESTORS SPEAK TO HIM FROM THE SHADOWS:
"BATTLE IS THE HONORABLE THING!" THEY CRY. "TO DIE IN BATTLE IS TO DIE A HERO!"
A HERO... TO WHOM, WHEN THERE ARE NONE LEFT TO REMEMBER?
IF ONLY HE COULD HAVE LED HIS CLAN TO SAFETY...! IF HE COULD EVEN HAVE SAVED LINA...! IF...! IF! IF! IF!
"COME BACK TO ME, ALONE IF YOU MUST! COME BACK TO ME...!"
HE HEARS FOOTSTEPS, AND FOR A MOMENT HE BELIEVES THE BATTLE HAS FOUND HIM.
HE WILL LOOK LIKE A COWARD, HIDING IN THE HALLS!
BUT IT'S ONLY THE SPRIGGAN, UNGT, WHO STOPS IN HIS TRACKS AND STARES AT HIM BLANKLY.
UNGT'S BODY QUIVERS...
...AND FALLS.
"SUCH IS THE FATE OF THOSE WHO FLEE." TIROL THINKS, AND THE DECISION IS MADE.

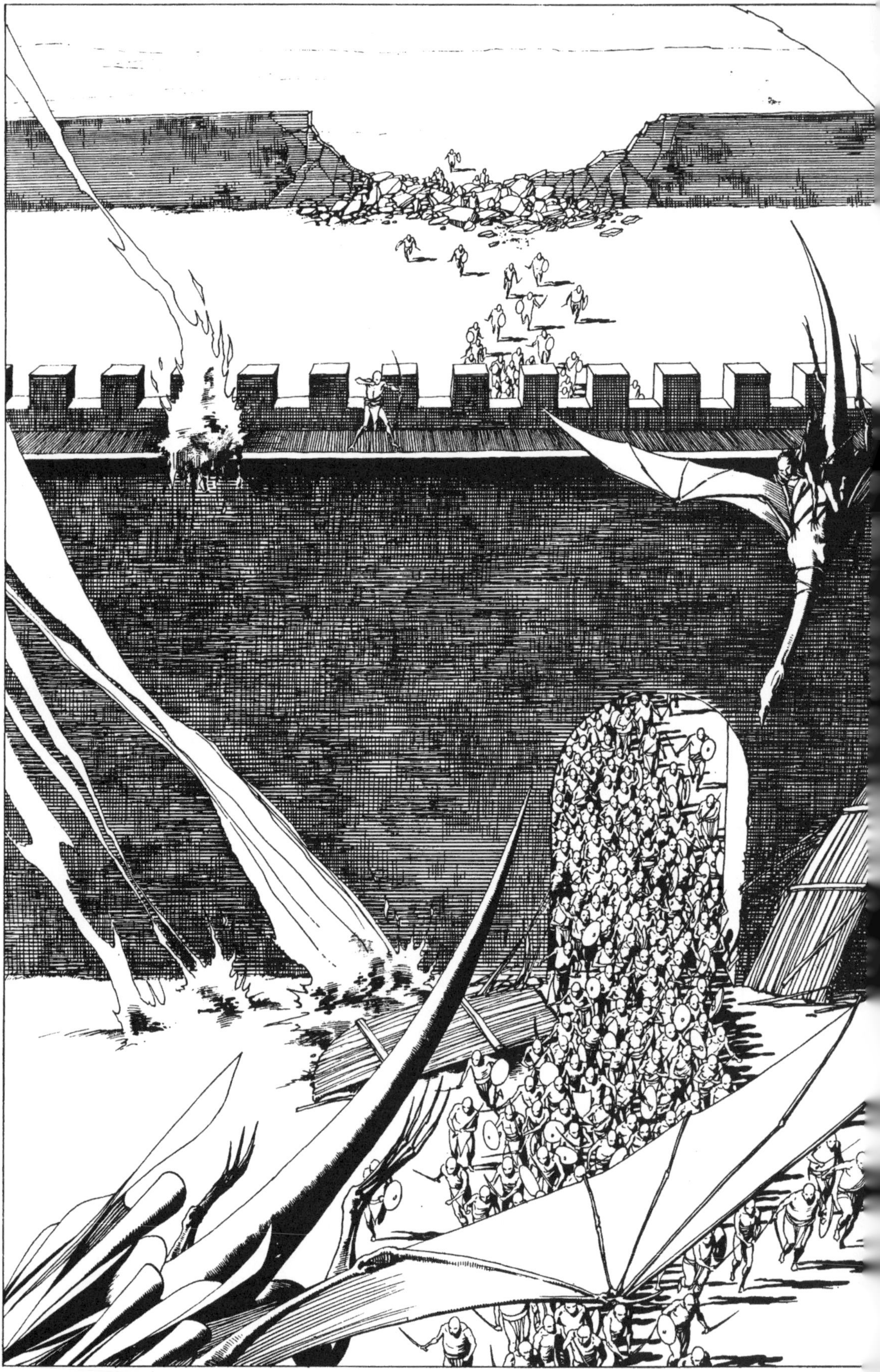

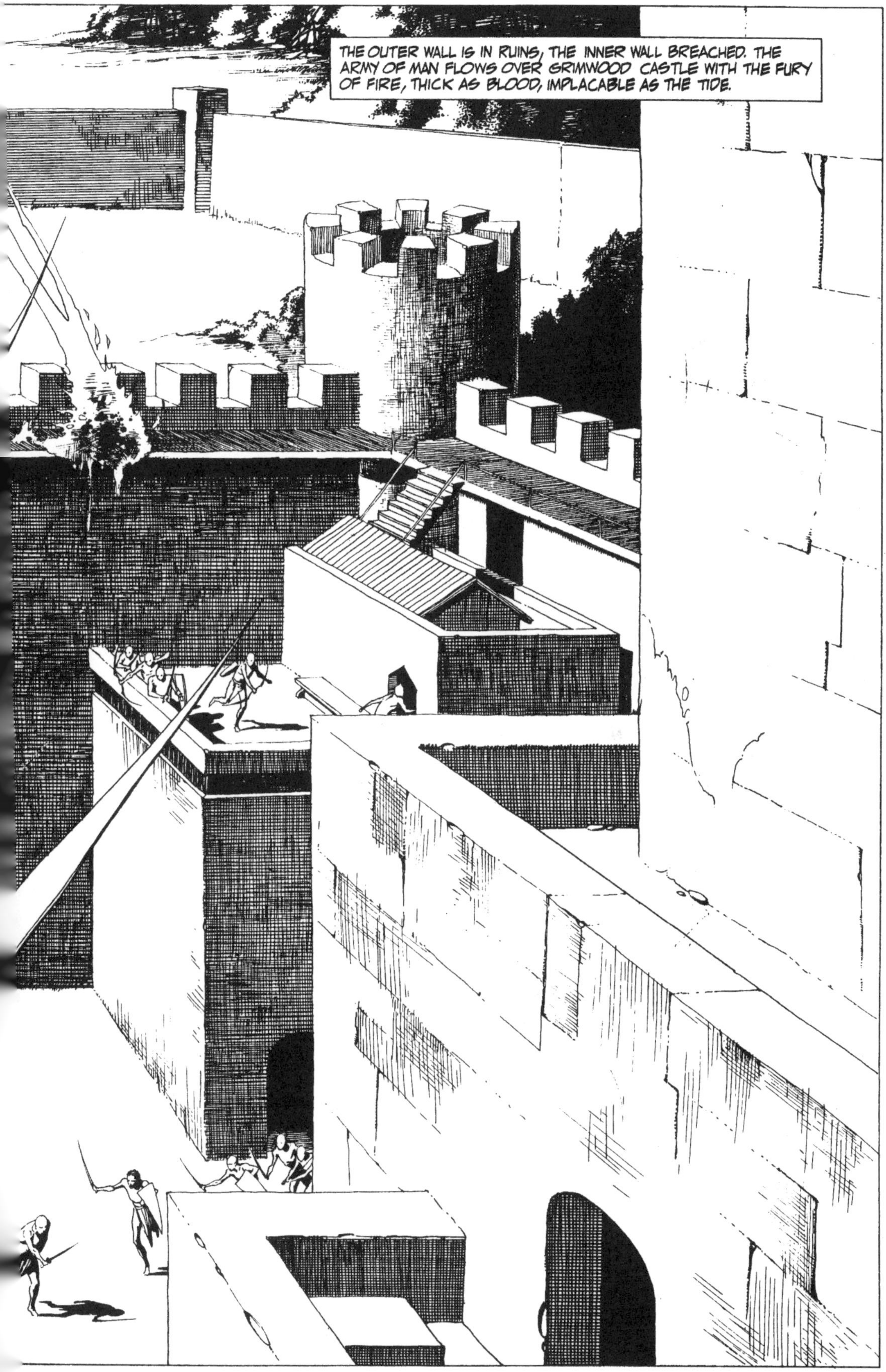
THE OUTER WALL IS IN RUINS, THE INNER WALL BREACHED. THE ARMY OF MAN FLOWS OVER GRIMWOOD CASTLE WITH THE FURY OF FIRE, THICK AS BLOOD, IMPLACABLE AS THE TIDE.

THE CASTLE ITSELF IS VIOLATED AND MEN SPREAD THROUGH ITS ROOMS AND HALLS LIKE A VIRULENT DISEASE.

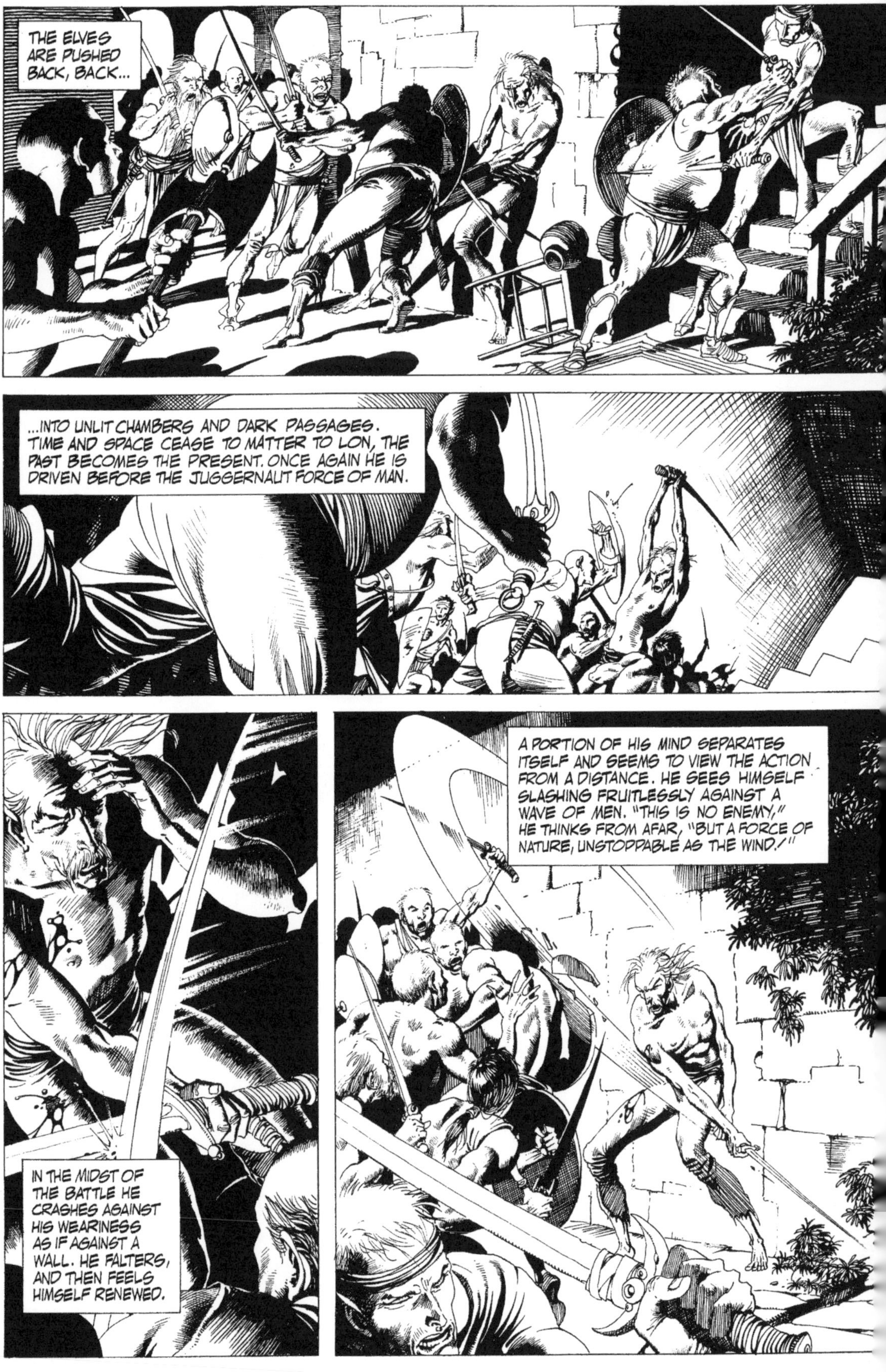
THE ELVES ARE PUSHED BACK, BACK...
...INTO UNLIT CHAMBERS AND DARK PASSAGES. TIME AND SPACE CEASE TO MATTER TO LON, THE PAST BECOMES THE PRESENT. ONCE AGAIN HE IS DRIVEN BEFORE THE JUGGERNAUT FORCE OF MAN.
IN THE MIDST OF THE BATTLE HE CRASHES AGAINST HIS WEARINESS AS IF AGAINST A WALL. HE FALTERS, AND THEN FEELS HIMSELF RENEWED.
A PORTION OF HIS MIND SEPARATES ITSELF AND SEEMS TO VIEW THE ACTION FROM A DISTANCE. HE SEES HIMSELF SLASHING FRUITLESSLY AGAINST A WAVE OF MEN. "THIS IS NO ENEMY," HE THINKS FROM AFAR, "BUT A FORCE OF NATURE, UNSTOPPABLE AS THE WIND!"

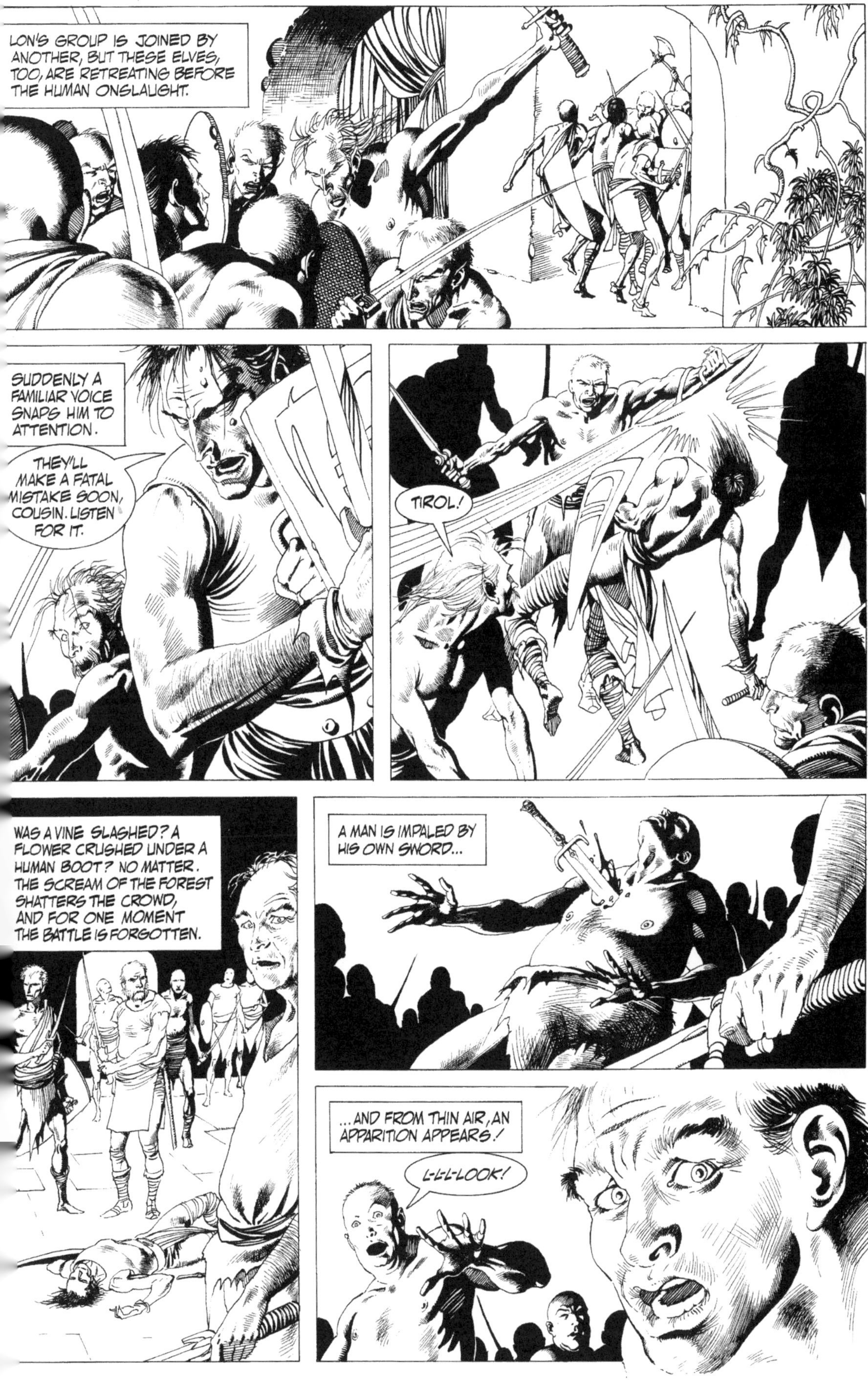

LON'S GROUP IS JOINED BY ANOTHER, BUT THESE ELVES, TOO, ARE RETREATING BEFORE THE HUMAN ONSLAUGHT.
SUDDENLY A FAMILIAR VOICE SNAPS HIM TO ATTENTION.
THEY'LL MAKE A FATAL MISTAKE SOON, COUSIN. LISTEN FOR IT.
TIROL!
WAS A VINE SLASHED? A FLOWER CRUSHED UNDER A HUMAN BOOT? NO MATTER. THE SCREAM OF THE FOREST SHATTERS THE CROWD, AND FOR ONE MOMENT THE BATTLE IS FORGOTTEN.
A MAN IS IMPALED BY HIS OWN SWORD...
...AND FROM THIN AIR, AN APPARITION APPEARS!
L-L-L-LOOK!

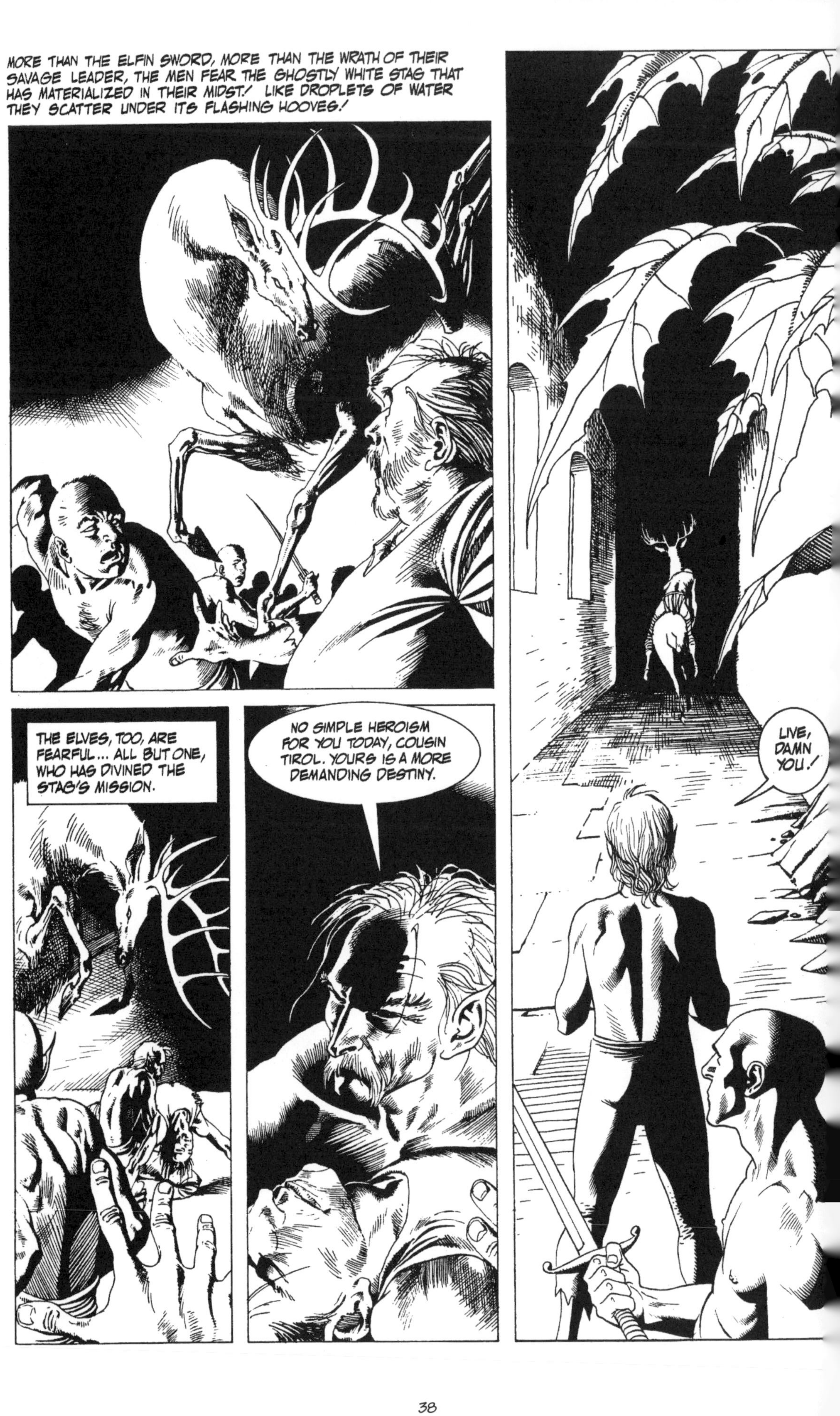
MORE THAN THE ELFIN SWORD, MORE THAN THE WRATH OF THEIR SAVAGE LEADER, THE MEN FEAR THE GHOSTLY WHITE STAG THAT HAS MATERIALIZED IN THEIR MIDST! LIKE DROPLETS OF WATER THEY SCATTER UNDER ITS FLASHING HOOVES!
THE ELVES, TOO, ARE FEARFUL... ALL BUT ONE, WHO HAS DIVINED THE STAG'S MISSION.
NO SIMPLE HEROISM FOR YOU TODAY, COUSIN TIROL. YOURS IS A MORE DEMANDING DESTINY.
LIVE, DAMN YOU!

GRIMWOOD'S DAUGHTER

HAPTER FIVE

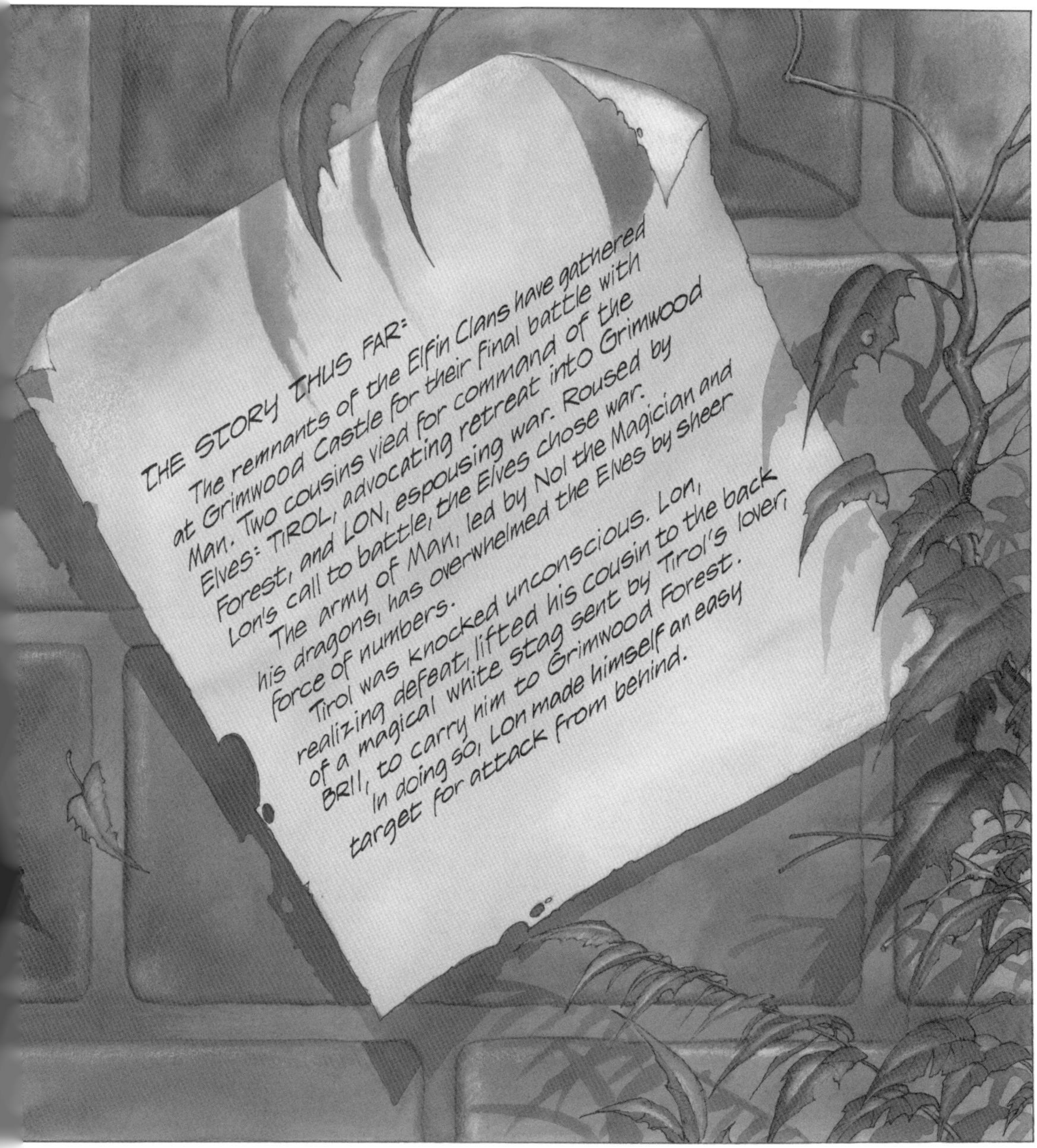
THE STORY THUS FAR:
The remnants of the Elfin Clans have gathered at Grimwood Castle for their final battle with Man. Two cousins vied for command of the Elves: TIROL, advocating retreat into Grimwood Forest, and LON, espousing war. Roused by Lon's call to battle, the Elves chose war.
The army of Man, led by Nol the Magician and his dragons, has overwhelmed the Elves by sheer force of numbers.
Tirol was knocked unconscious. Lon, realizing defeat, lifted his cousin to the back of a magical white stag sent by Tirol's lover, BRII, to carry him to Grimwood Forest.
In doing so, Lon made himself an easy target for attack from behind.

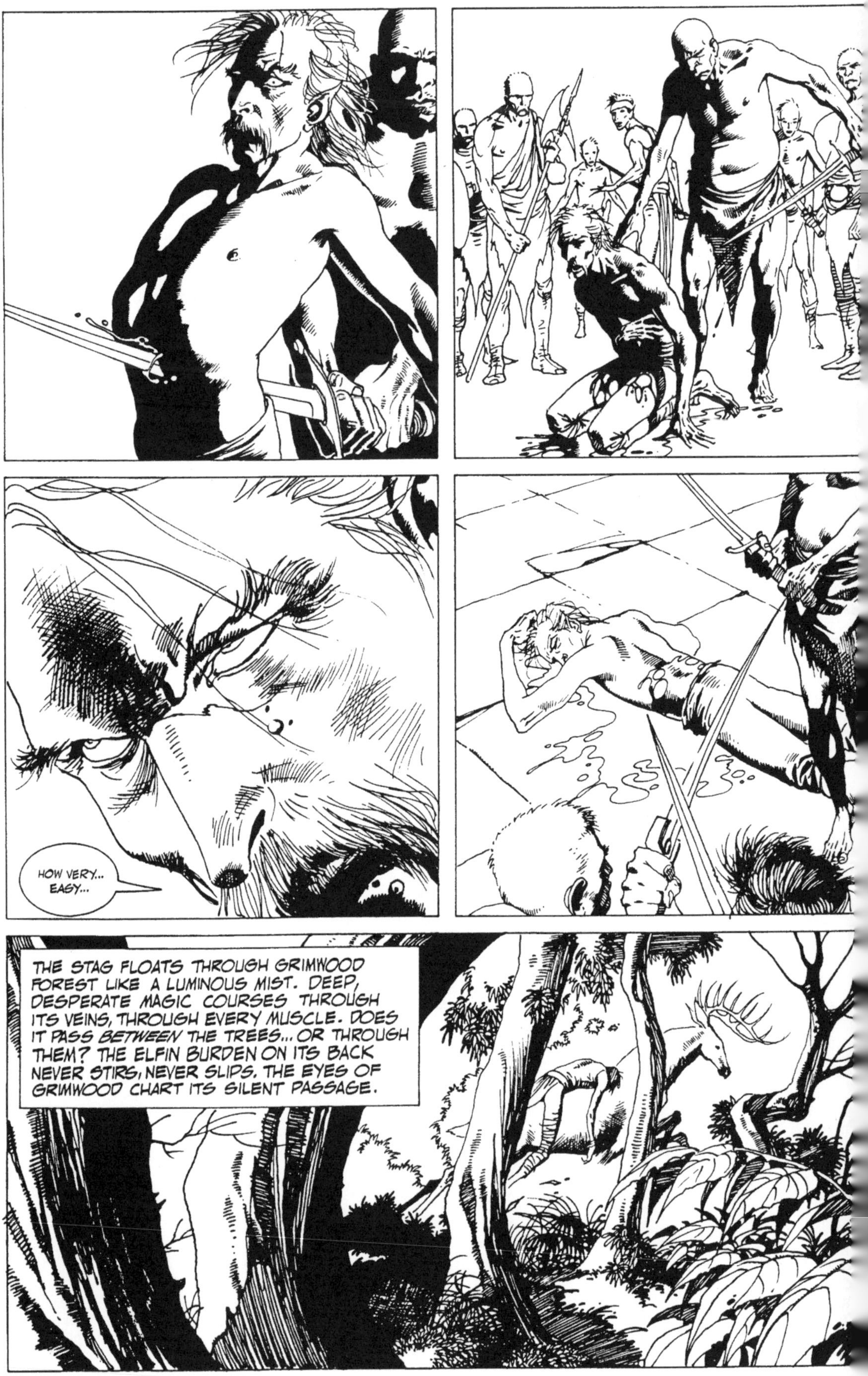
HOW VERY... EASY...
THE STAG FLOATS THROUGH GRIMWOOD FOREST LIKE A LUMINOUS MIST. DEEP, DESPERATE MAGIC COURSES THROUGH ITS VEINS, THROUGH EVERY MUSCLE. DOES IT PASS *BETWEEN* THE TREES... OR THROUGH THEM? THE ELFIN BURDEN ON ITS BACK NEVER STIRS, NEVER SLIPS. THE EYES OF GRIMWOOD CHART ITS SILENT PASSAGE.

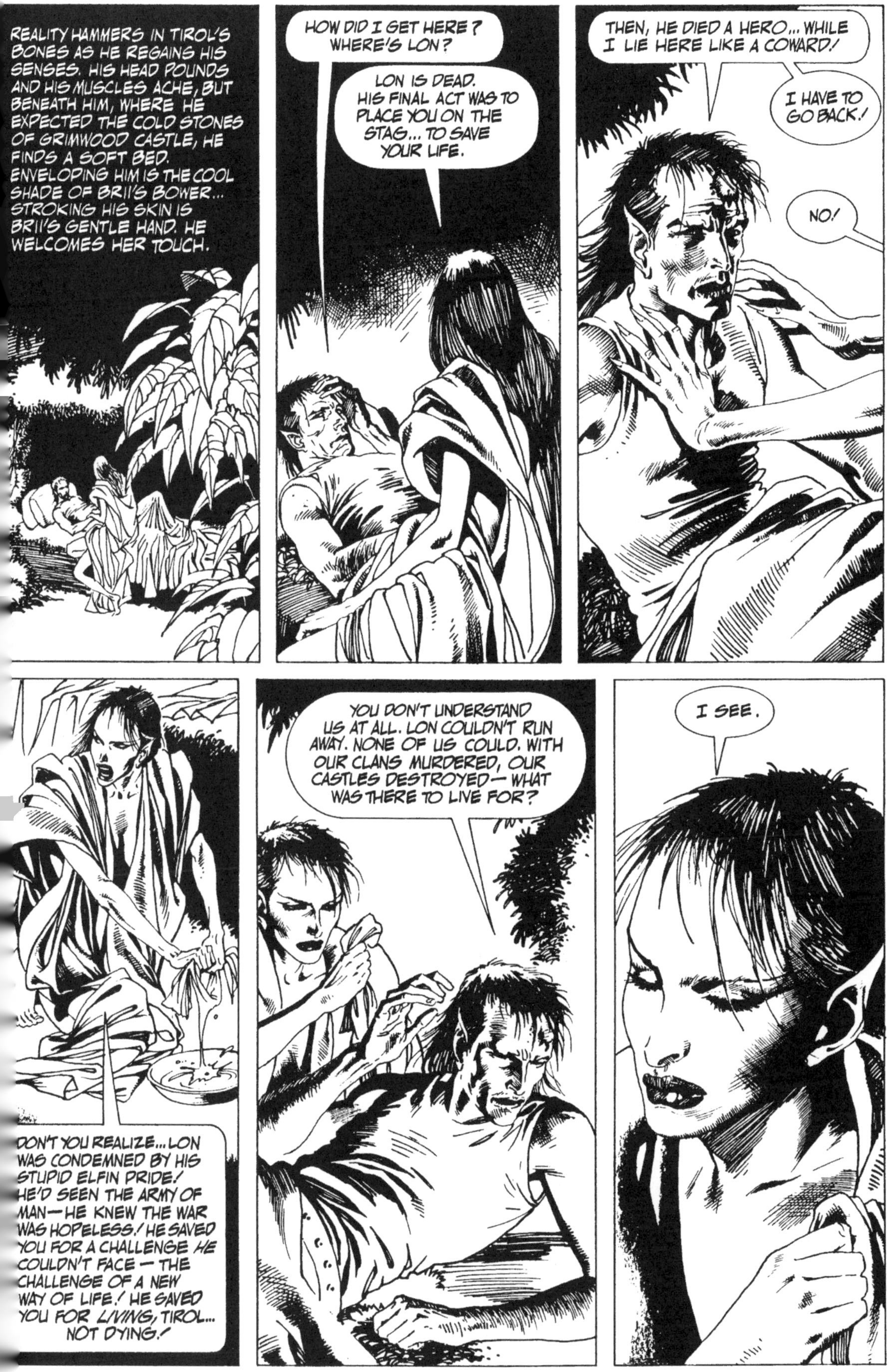
REALITY HAMMERS IN TIROL'S BONES AS HE REGAINS HIS SENSES. HIS HEAD POUNDS AND HIS MUSCLES ACHE, BUT BENEATH HIM, WHERE HE EXPECTED THE COLD STONES OF GRIMWOOD CASTLE, HE FINDS A SOFT BED. ENVELOPING HIM IS THE COOL SHADE OF BRII'S BOWER... STROKING HIS SKIN IS BRII'S GENTLE HAND. HE WELCOMES HER TOUCH.
HOW DID I GET HERE? WHERE'S LON?
LON IS DEAD. HIS FINAL ACT WAS TO PLACE YOU ON THE STAG... TO SAVE YOUR LIFE.
THEN, HE DIED A HERO... WHILE I LIE HERE LIKE A COWARD!
I HAVE TO GO BACK!
NO!
DON'T YOU REALIZE... LON WAS CONDEMNED BY HIS STUPID ELFIN PRIDE! HE'D SEEN THE ARMY OF MAN—HE KNEW THE WAR WAS HOPELESS! HE SAVED YOU FOR A CHALLENGE HE COULDN'T FACE — THE CHALLENGE OF A NEW WAY OF LIFE! HE SAVED YOU FOR LIVING, TIROL... NOT DYING!
YOU DON'T UNDERSTAND US AT ALL. LON COULDN'T RUN AWAY. NONE OF US COULD. WITH OUR CLANS MURDERED, OUR CASTLES DESTROYED— WHAT WAS THERE TO LIVE FOR?
I SEE.

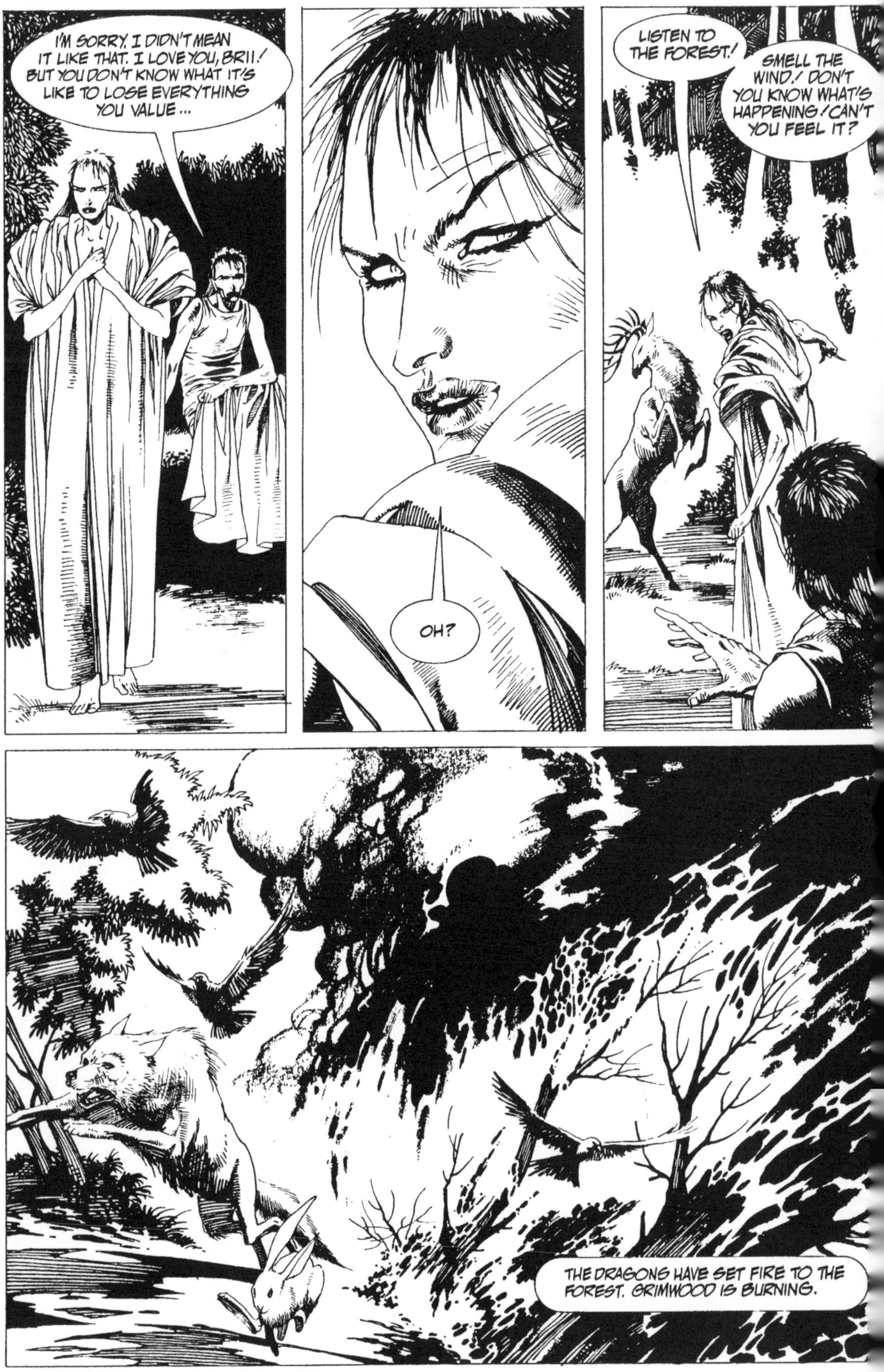
I'M SORRY. I DIDN'T MEAN IT LIKE THAT. I LOVE YOU, BRII! BUT YOU DON'T KNOW WHAT IT'S LIKE TO LOSE EVERYTHING YOU VALUE ...
OH?
LISTEN TO THE FOREST!
SMELL THE WIND! DON'T YOU KNOW WHAT'S HAPPENING? CAN'T YOU FEEL IT?
THE DRAGONS HAVE SET FIRE TO THE FOREST. GRIMWOOD IS BURNING.

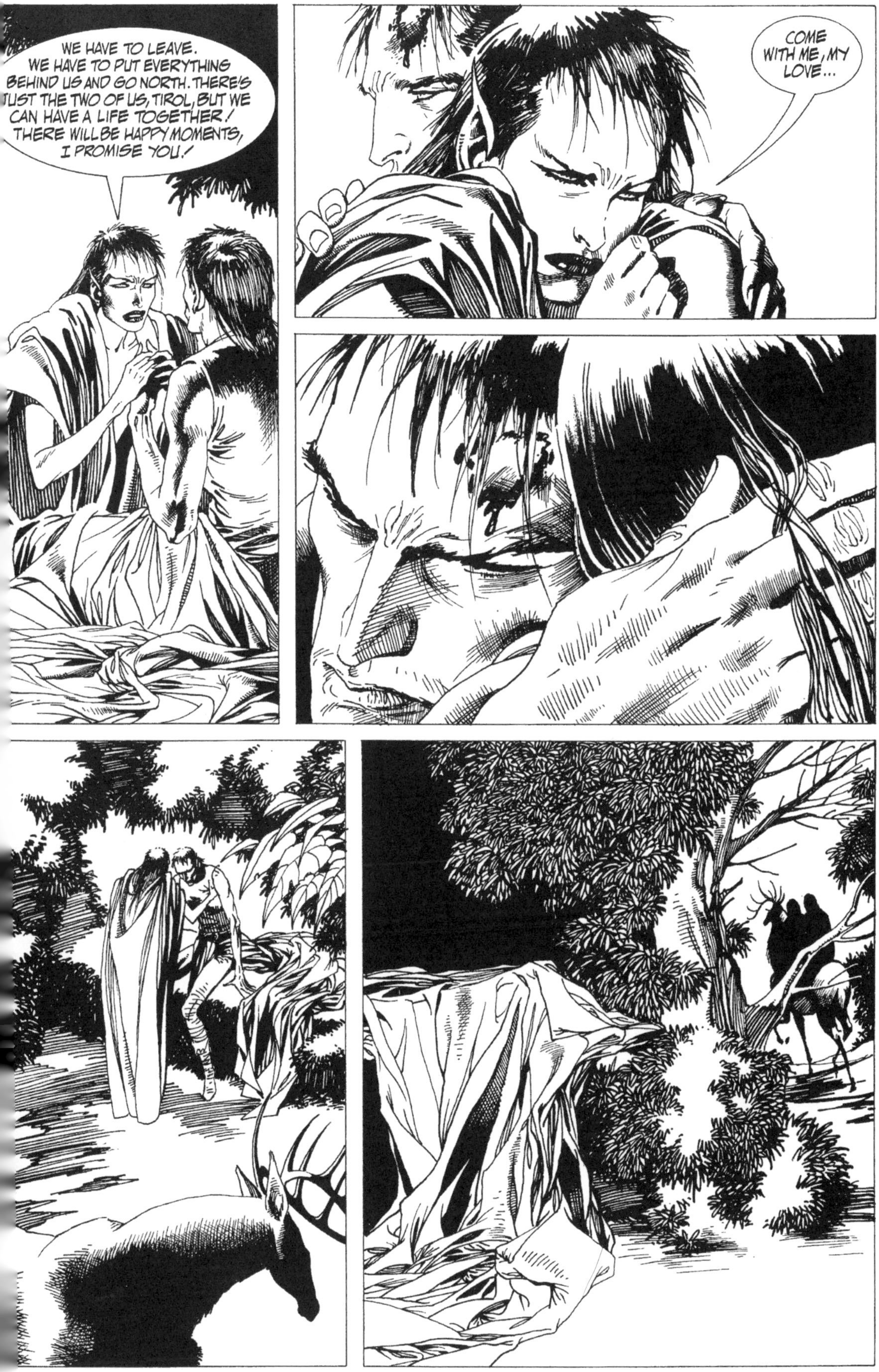
WE HAVE TO LEAVE. WE HAVE TO PUT EVERYTHING BEHIND US AND GO NORTH. THERE'S JUST THE TWO OF US, TIROL, BUT WE CAN HAVE A LIFE TOGETHER! THERE WILL BE HAPPY MOMENTS, I PROMISE YOU!
COME WITH ME, MY LOVE...

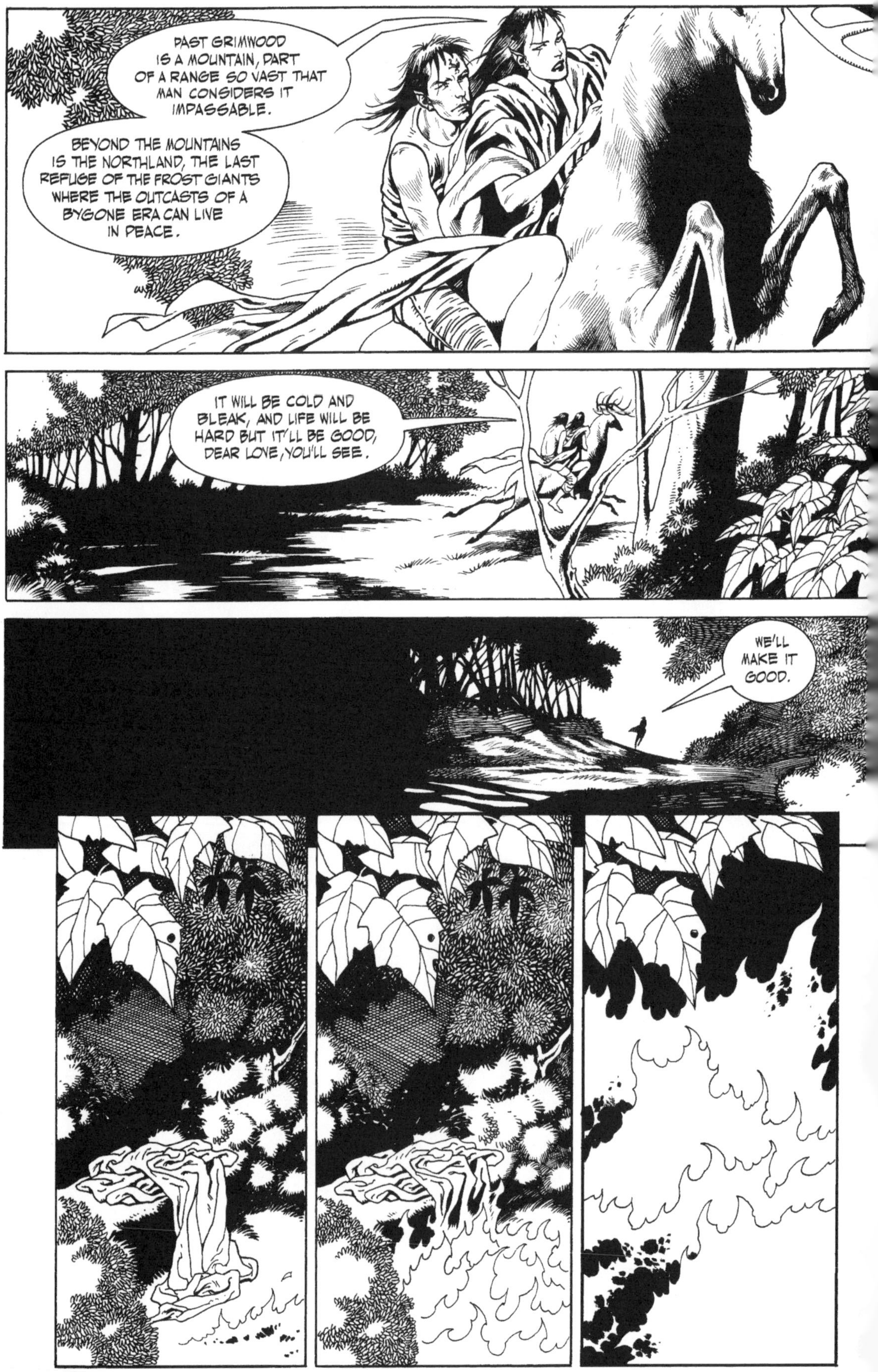
PAST GRIMWOOD IS A MOUNTAIN, PART OF A RANGE SO VAST THAT MAN CONSIDERS IT IMPASSABLE.
BEYOND THE MOUNTAINS IS THE NORTHLAND, THE LAST REFUGE OF THE FROST GIANTS WHERE THE OUTCASTS OF A BYGONE ERA CAN LIVE IN PEACE.
IT WILL BE COLD AND BLEAK, AND LIFE WILL BE HARD BUT IT'LL BE GOOD, DEAR LOVE, YOU'LL SEE.
WE'LL MAKE IT GOOD.

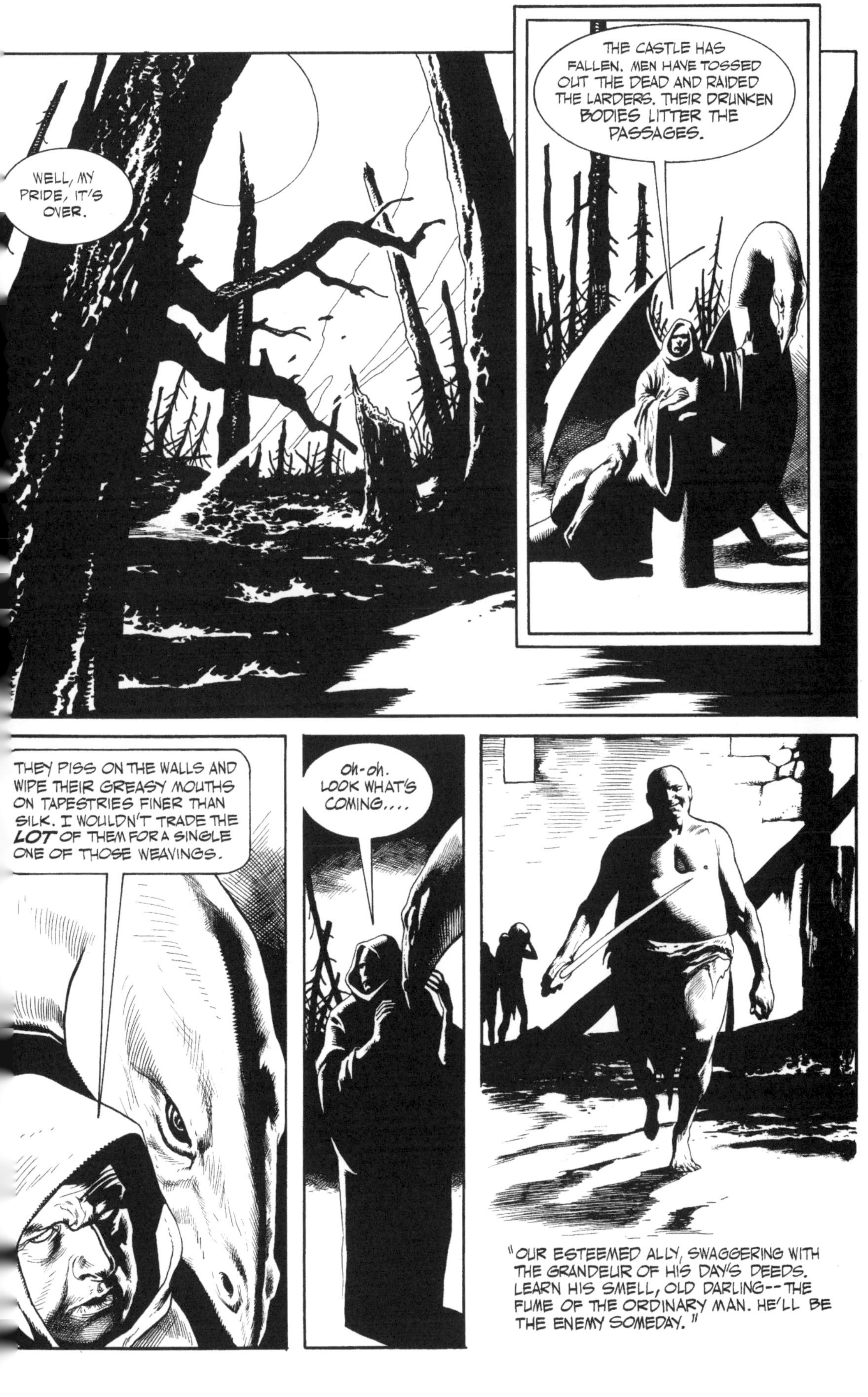
WELL, MY PRIDE, IT'S OVER.
THE CASTLE HAS FALLEN. MEN HAVE TOSSED OUT THE DEAD AND RAIDED THE LARDERS. THEIR DRUNKEN BODIES LITTER THE PASSAGES.
THEY PISS ON THE WALLS AND WIPE THEIR GREASY MOUTHS ON TAPESTRIES FINER THAN SILK. I WOULDN'T TRADE THE **LOT** OF THEM FOR A SINGLE ONE OF THOSE WEAVINGS.
Oh-oh. LOOK WHAT'S COMING....
"OUR ESTEEMED ALLY, SWAGGERING WITH THE GRANDEUR OF HIS DAY'S DEEDS. LEARN HIS SMELL, OLD DARLING--THE FUME OF THE ORDINARY MAN. HE'LL BE THE ENEMY SOMEDAY."

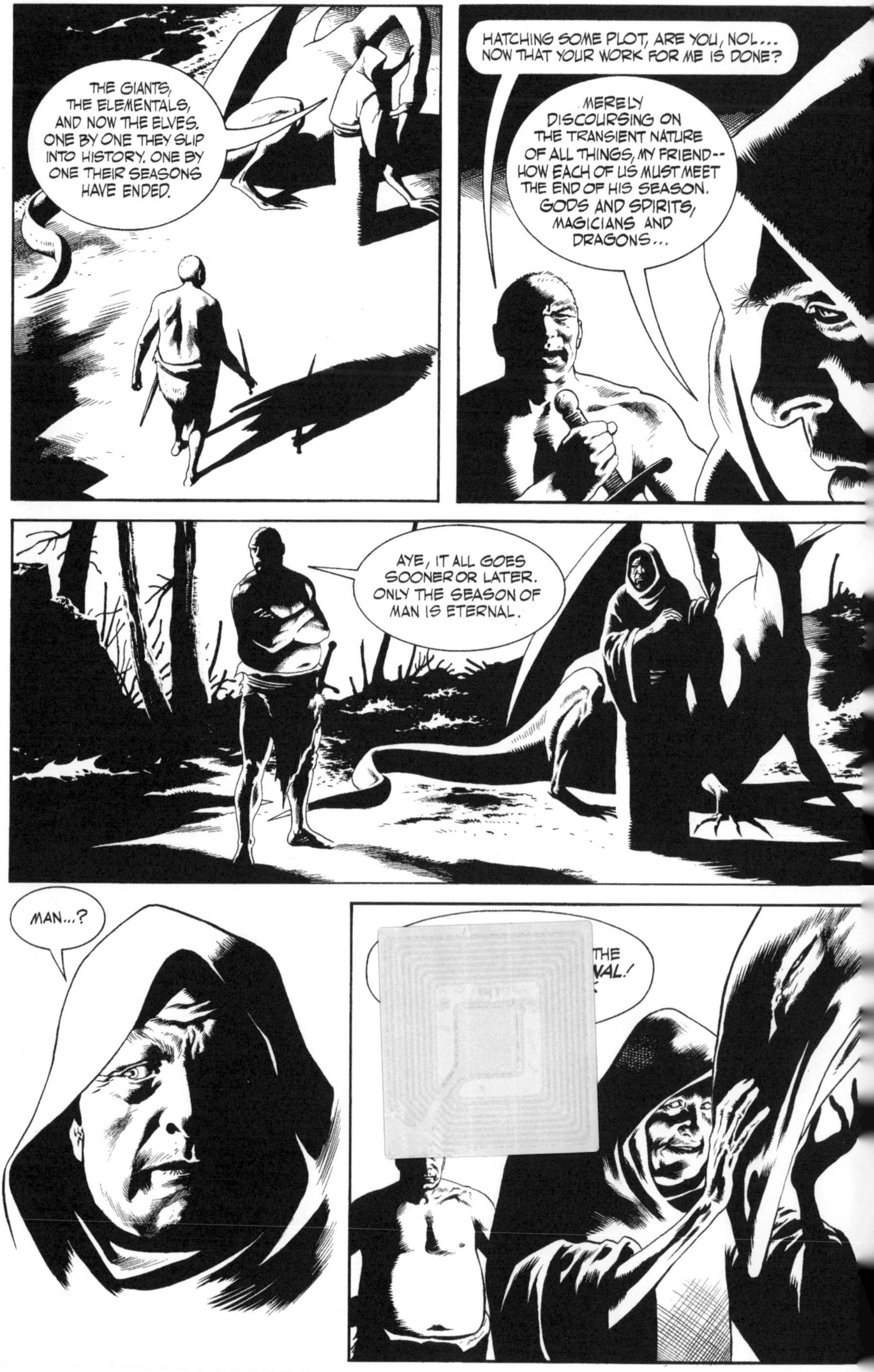
THE GIANTS, THE ELEMENTALS, AND NOW THE ELVES. ONE BY ONE THEY SLIP INTO HISTORY. ONE BY ONE THEIR SEASONS HAVE ENDED.
HATCHING SOME PLOT, ARE YOU, NOL... NOW THAT YOUR WORK FOR ME IS DONE?
MERELY DISCOURSING ON THE TRANSIENT NATURE OF ALL THINGS, MY FRIEND-- HOW EACH OF US MUST MEET THE END OF HIS SEASON. GODS AND SPIRITS, MAGICIANS AND DRAGONS...
AYE, IT ALL GOES SOONER OR LATER. ONLY THE SEASON OF MAN IS ETERNAL.
MAN...?

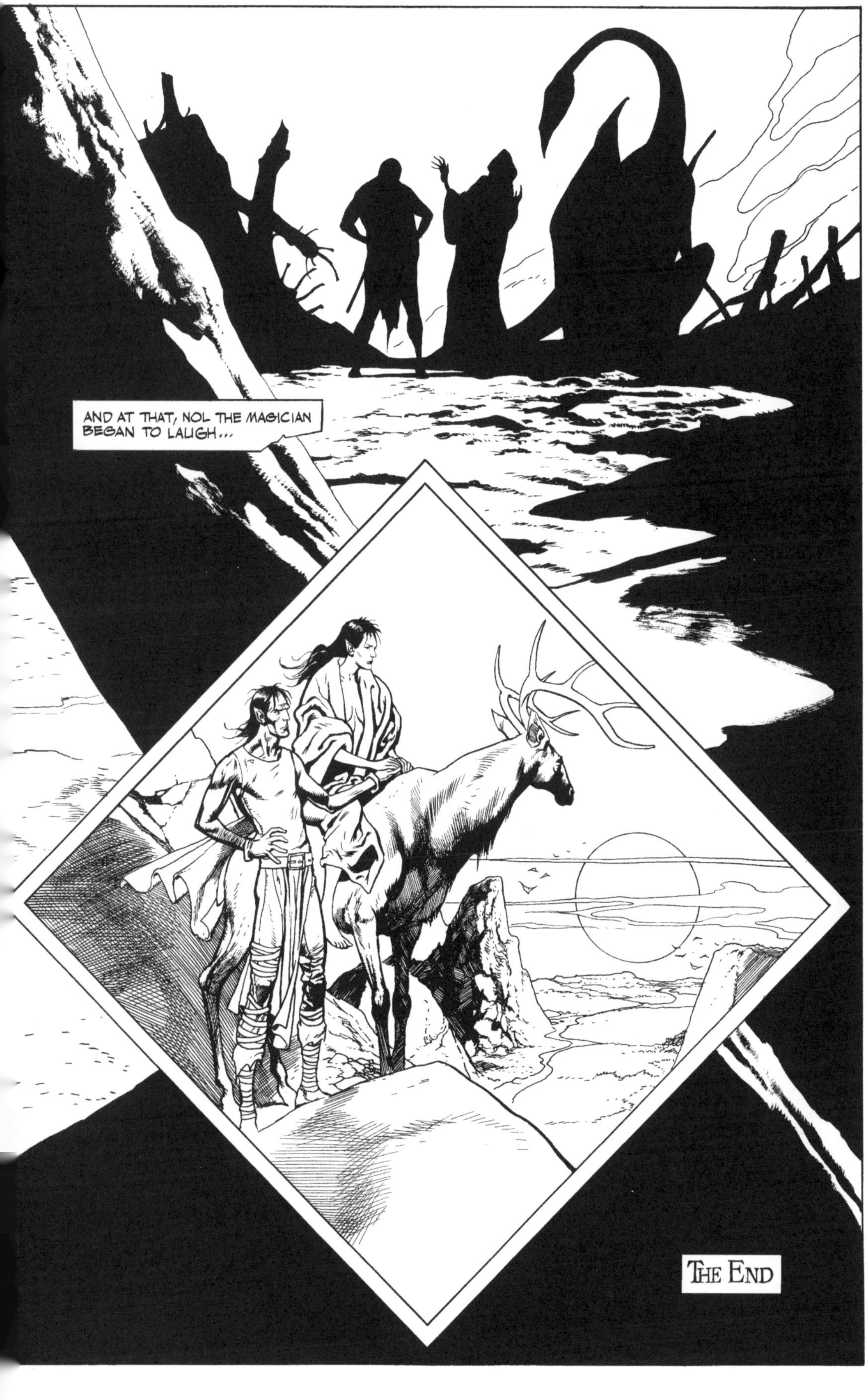
AND AT THAT, NOL THE MAGICIAN BEGAN TO LAUGH...
THE END

BONUS MATERIAL

Presenting a selection of *Grimwood's Daughter* sketches and preliminaries by **Kevin Nowlan.**

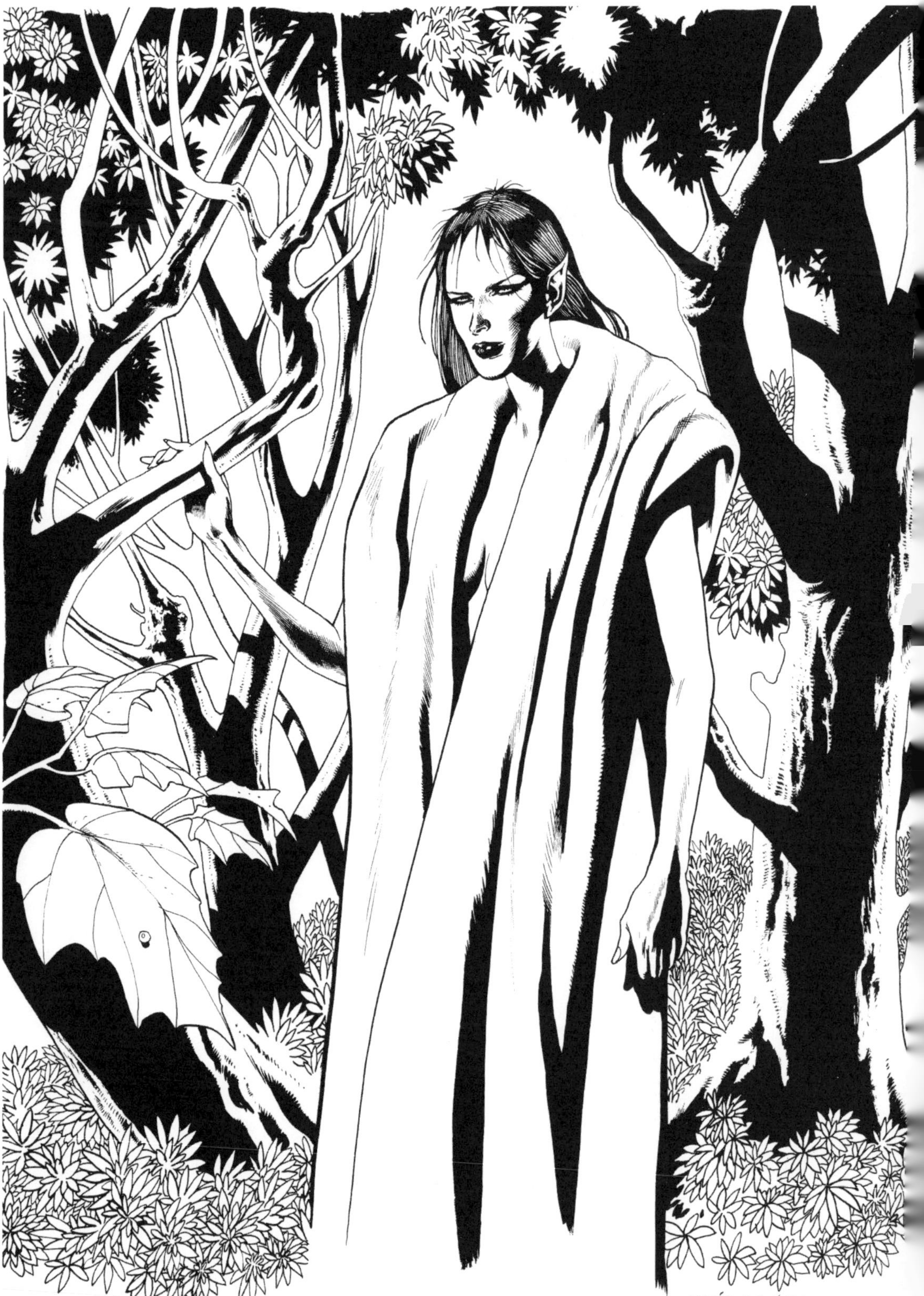
Kevin Nowlan

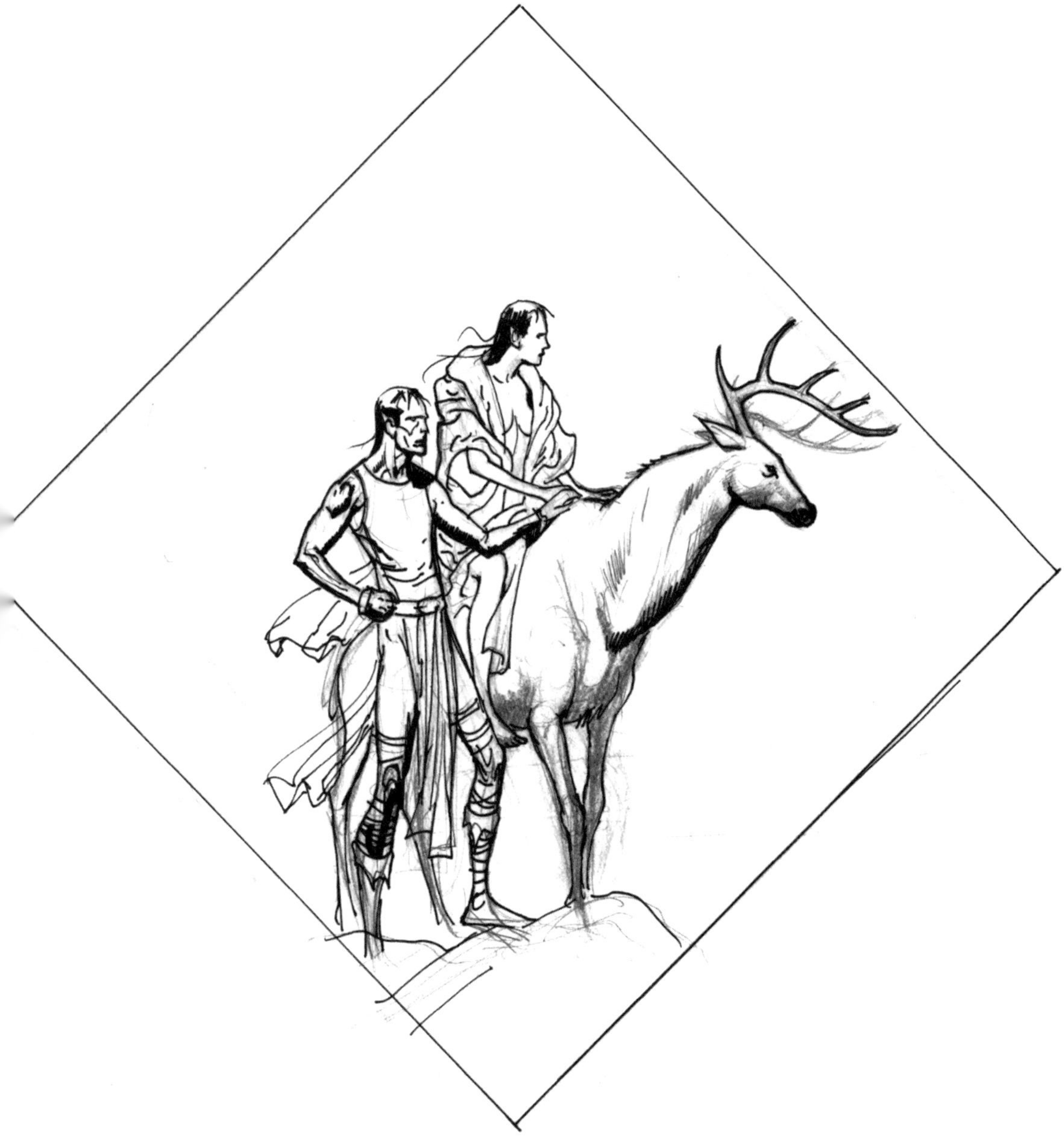

TWO (10)

UNEVEN DOUBLE LIGHTING

THREE (11)

THREE

1. FOUR SHOT ELF W/ FOOT OUT
2. FOUR SHOT LAUGHING @ FALLEN KID
3. TIROL SPEAKING, ANNOYED FACES BEHIND HIM
4. FAMILY & TUB OF WATER W/ CHEESE
5. FARMER & CHILDREN GAWK @ 2 HEAD CALF
6. GROUND SHOT, WITHERED CROPS, DESOLATE FAR

FOUR

1. ELF RIDES FROM CRUDE HUT
2. MAGICIAN CASTING SPELL OR SOMETHING
3. TIROL SPEAKING, BIG BALLOON, ANGRY, ASHAMED, SCOWLING FACES
4. BIG PANEL - BATTLE, NOL ON DRAGON, DRAGONS IN SKY - FIGHTING ELVES & MEN

FOUR (12)

FIVE (13)

FIVE (13)

1. ONE SHOT OF TIROL TALKING (FRONT)
2. LON POUNDS TABLE "NO"
3. " STANDS, GIVES SPEECH
4. GRUM. & UNGT, GRUM CHOKING, UNGT SUR BALLOON OFF PANEL
5. LON WALKING ABOUT, PSYCHING UP THE
6. TIROL LEANS BACK WEARILY (CLOSE SH "SAME OLD LON

SIX (14)

1. LONG SHOT OF ELVES TALKING, AROUN (CAPTION)
2. GRUM. & UNGT SLEEP IN FG. LON ST IN BG. OTHER ELVES WEARY. LON SPE (ALSO CAPTION)
3. OUTSIDE WINDOW - TIROL LOOKS OU LON & ELVES WAIT FOR HIS RESPON
4. CLOSE ON TIROL, RUBS FOREHEA
5. LONG SHOT OF CASTLE. BALLOON

SIX (14)

SEVEN (15)

SEVEN (15)

1. LON IN FG. WATCHING TIR. LEAVE HALL. (CAPTION)
2. CLOSE ON LON, THINKING (THOUGHT BALLOON)
3. LON FOLLOWING TIR. (NOW W/ CAP THRU CORRIDORS. (BIG CAPTION)
4. LON RUNNING DOWN SHORT HALLWA @ END & OFF TO ONE SIDE, DOOR TO OUTSIDE, TIR. HAS GONE OUT, (CAPTION)
5. LON STANDS, ASTONISHED IN DOORWAY OUTSIDE - IT LEADS DOWN STEPS & INTO FOREST - TIROL ON BACK OF REARING WHITE STAG IN FG.

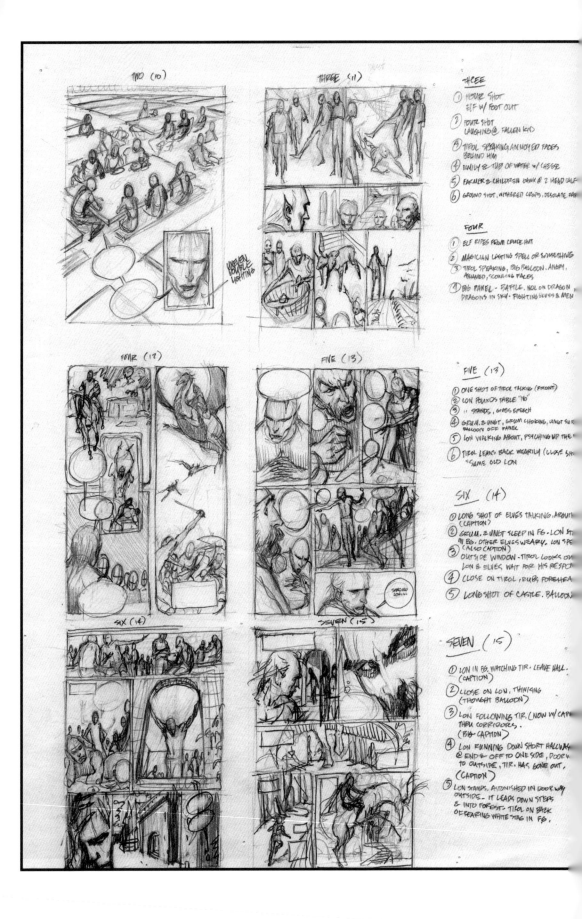

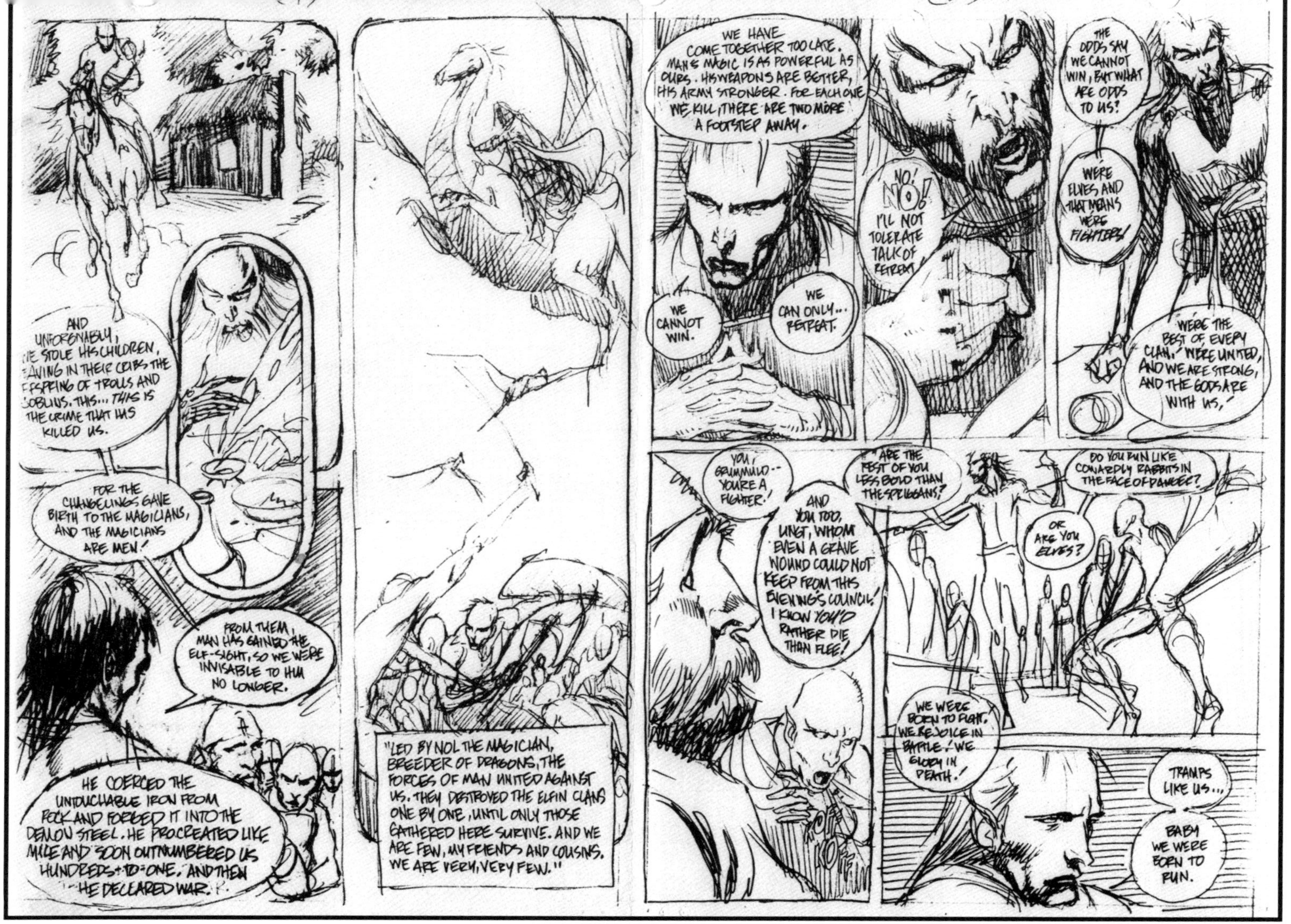
AND UNFORGIVABLY, HE STOLE HIS CHILDREN, LEAVING IN THEIR CRIBS THE OFFSPRING OF TROLLS AND GOBLINS. THIS... THIS IS THE CRIME THAT HAS KILLED US.
FOR THE CHANGELINGS GAVE BIRTH TO THE MAGICIANS, AND THE MAGICIANS ARE MEN!
FROM THEM, MAN HAS GAINED THE ELF-SIGHT, SO WE WERE INVISABLE TO HIM NO LONGER.
HE COERCED THE UNTOUCHABLE IRON FROM ROCK AND FORGED IT INTO THE DEMON STEEL. HE PROCREATED LIKE MICE AND SOON OUTNUMBERED US HUNDREDS-TO-ONE, AND THEN HE DECLARED WAR.
"LED BY NOL THE MAGICIAN, BREEDER OF DRAGONS, THE FORCES OF MAN UNITED AGAINST US. THEY DESTROYED THE ELFIN CLANS ONE BY ONE, UNTIL ONLY THOSE GATHERED HERE SURVIVE. AND WE ARE FEW, MY FRIENDS AND COUSINS. WE ARE VERY, VERY FEW."
WE HAVE COME TOGETHER TOO LATE. MAN'S MAGIC IS AS POWERFUL AS OURS. HIS WEAPONS ARE BETTER, HIS ARMY STRONGER. FOR EACH ONE WE KILL, THERE ARE TWO MORE A FOOTSTEP AWAY.
WE CANNOT WIN.
WE CAN ONLY... RETREAT.
NO! NO! I'LL NOT TOLERATE TALK OF RETREAT.
THE ODDS SAY WE CANNOT WIN, BUT WHAT ARE ODDS TO US?
WE'RE ELVES, AND THAT MEANS WE'RE FIGHTERS!
WE'RE THE BEST OF EVERY CLAN. WE'RE UNITED, AND WE ARE STRONG, AND THE GODS ARE WITH US.
YOU, GRIMMULD-- YOU'RE A FIGHTER!
AND YOU TOO, UNGT, WHOM EVEN A GRAVE WOUND COULD NOT KEEP FROM THIS EVENING'S COUNCIL! I KNOW YOU'D RATHER DIE THAN FLEE!
ARE THE REST OF YOU LESS BOLD THAN THE SPRIGGANS?
DO YOU RUN LIKE COWARDLY RABBITS IN THE FACE OF DANGER?
OR ARE YOU ELVES?
WE WERE BORN TO FIGHT. WE REJOICE IN BATTLE! WE GLORY IN DEATH!
TRAMPS LIKE US...
BABY WE WERE BORN TO RUN.

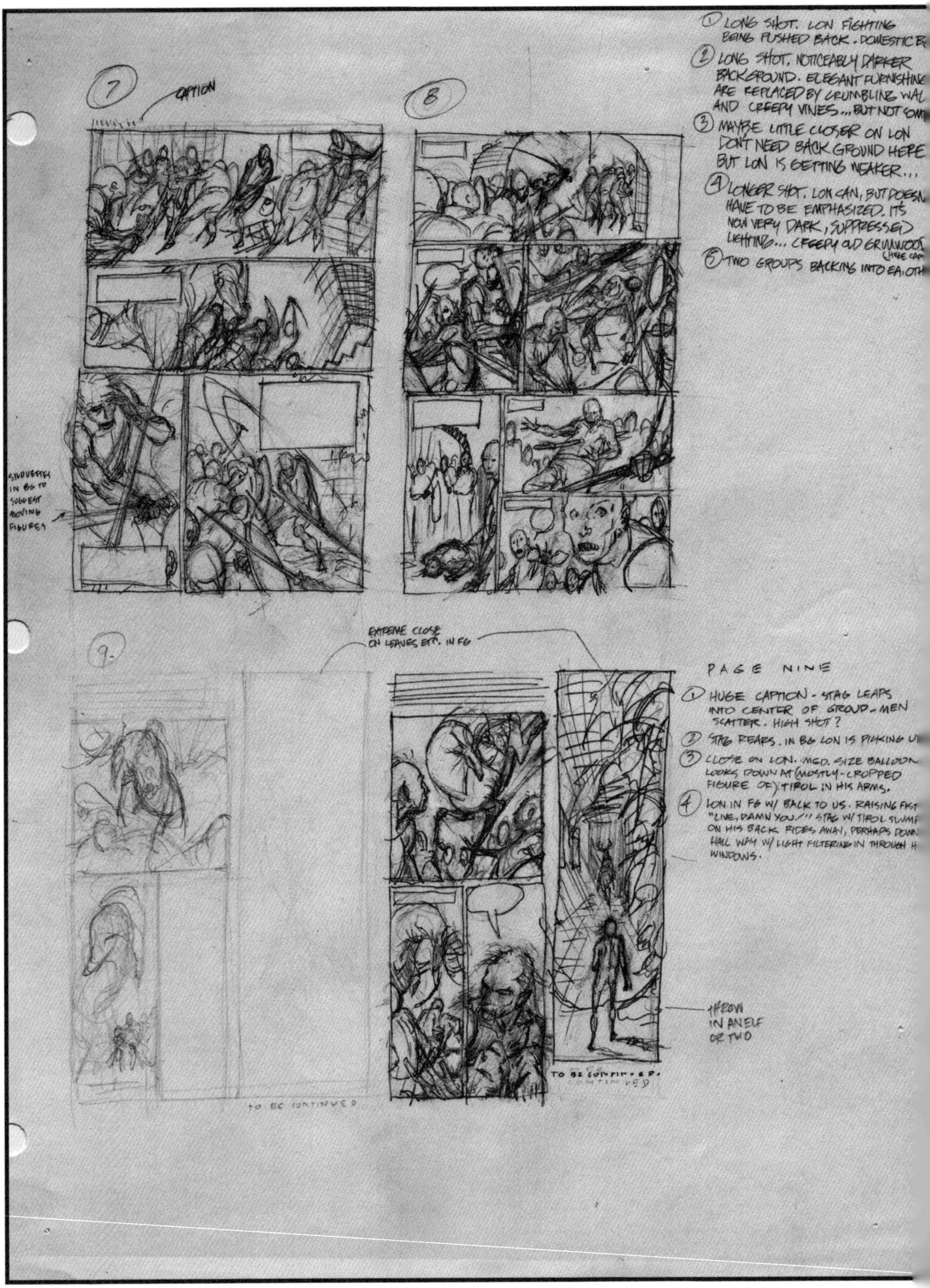
7
CAPTION
8
SILHOUETTES IN BG TO SUGGEST MOVING FIGURES
① LONG SHOT. LON FIGHTING BEING PUSHED BACK. DOMESTIC B
② LONG SHOT. NOTICEABLY DARKER BACKGROUND. ELEGANT FURNISHINGS ARE REPLACED BY CRUMBLING WAL AND CREEPY VINES... BUT NOT SOM
③ MAYBE LITTLE CLOSER ON LON DON'T NEED BACK GROUND HERE BUT LON IS GETTING WEAKER...
④ LONGER SHOT. LON CAN, BUT DOESN HAVE TO BE EMPHASIZED. IT'S NOW VERY DARK, SUPPRESSED LIGHTING... CREEPY OLD GRIMWOOD
(HUGE CAP
⑤ TWO GROUPS BACKING INTO EA. OTH
9.
EXTREME CLOSE ON LEAVES ETC. IN FG
TO BE CONTINUED
TO BE CONTINUED
PAGE NINE
① HUGE CAPTION - STAG LEAPS INTO CENTER OF GROUP - MEN SCATTER. HIGH SHOT?
② STAG REARS. IN BG LON IS PICKING U
③ CLOSE ON LON. MED. SIZE BALLOON LOOKS DOWN AT (MOSTLY-CROPPED FIGURE OF) TIROL IN HIS ARMS.
④ LON IN FG W/ BACK TO US. RAISING FIST "LIVE, DAMN YOU!" STAG W/ TIROL SLUMP ON HIS BACK RIDES AWAY, PERHAPS DOWN HALL WAY W/ LIGHT FILTERING IN THROUGH H WINDOWS.
THROW IN AN ELF OR TWO

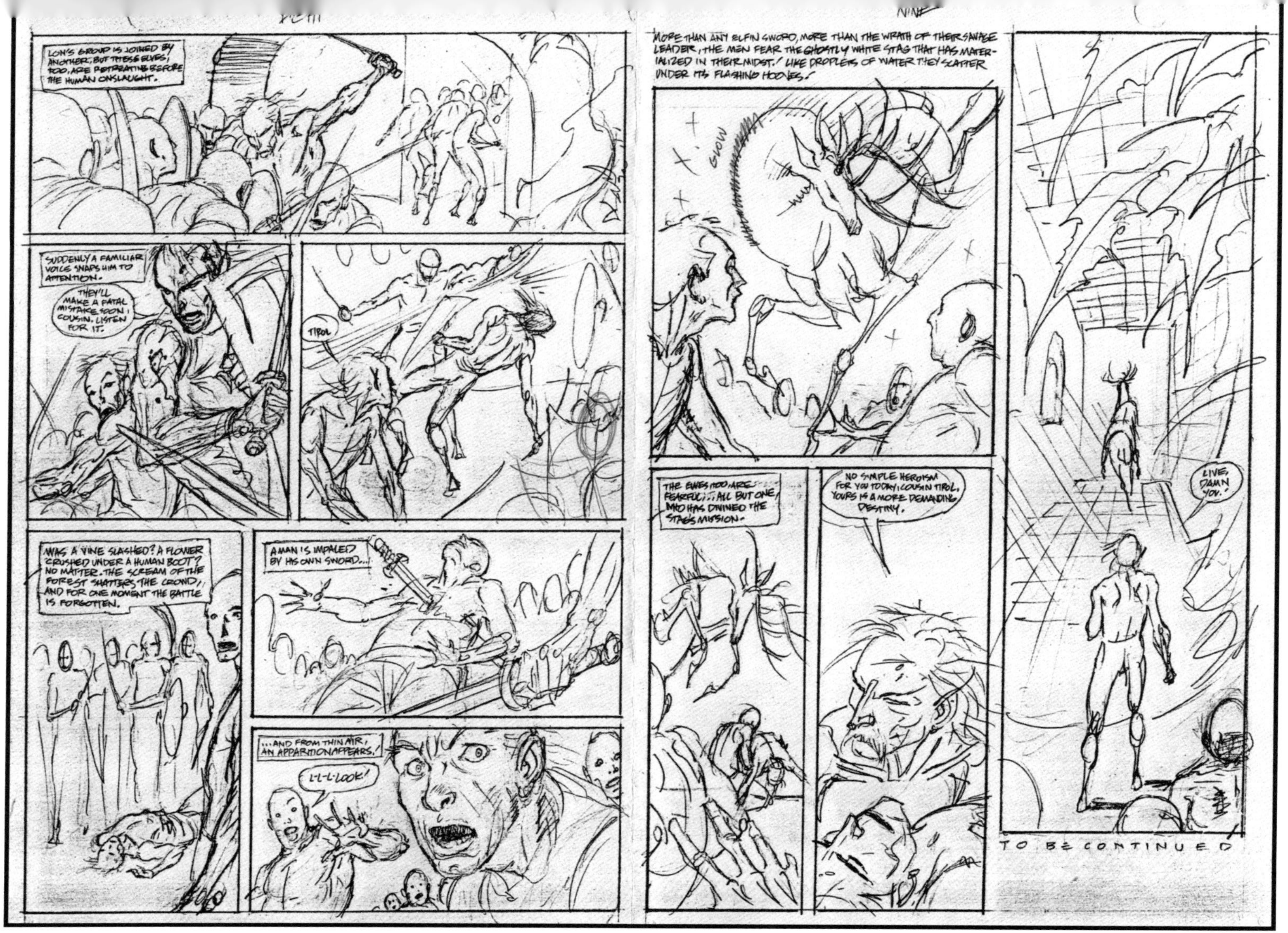
LON'S GROUP IS JOINED BY ANOTHER, BUT THESE ELVES, TOO, ARE RETREATING BEFORE THE HUMAN ONSLAUGHT.
SUDDENLY A FAMILIAR VOICE SNAPS HIM TO ATTENTION.
THEY'LL MAKE A FATAL MISTAKE SOON, COUSIN. LISTEN FOR IT.
TIROL
WAS A VINE SLASHED? A FLOWER CRUSHED UNDER A HUMAN BOOT? NO MATTER. THE SCREAM OF THE FOREST SHATTERS THE CROWD, AND FOR ONE MOMENT THE BATTLE IS FORGOTTEN.
A MAN IS IMPALED BY HIS OWN SWORD...
...AND FROM THIN AIR, AN APPARITION APPEARS.!
L-L-L-LOOK!
MORE THAN ANY ELFIN SWORD, MORE THAN THE WRATH OF THEIR SAVAGE LEADER, THE MEN FEAR THE GHOSTLY WHITE STAG THAT HAS MATERIALIZED IN THEIR MIDST.! LIKE DROPLETS OF WATER THEY SCATTER UNDER ITS FLASHING HOOVES.!
GLOW
THE ELVES, TOO, ARE FEARFUL... ALL BUT ONE, WHO HAS DIVINED THE STAG'S MISSION.
NO SIMPLE HEROISM FOR YOU TODAY, COUSIN TIROL. YOURS IS A MORE DEMANDING DESTINY.
LIVE, DAMN YOU.!
TO BE CONTINUED

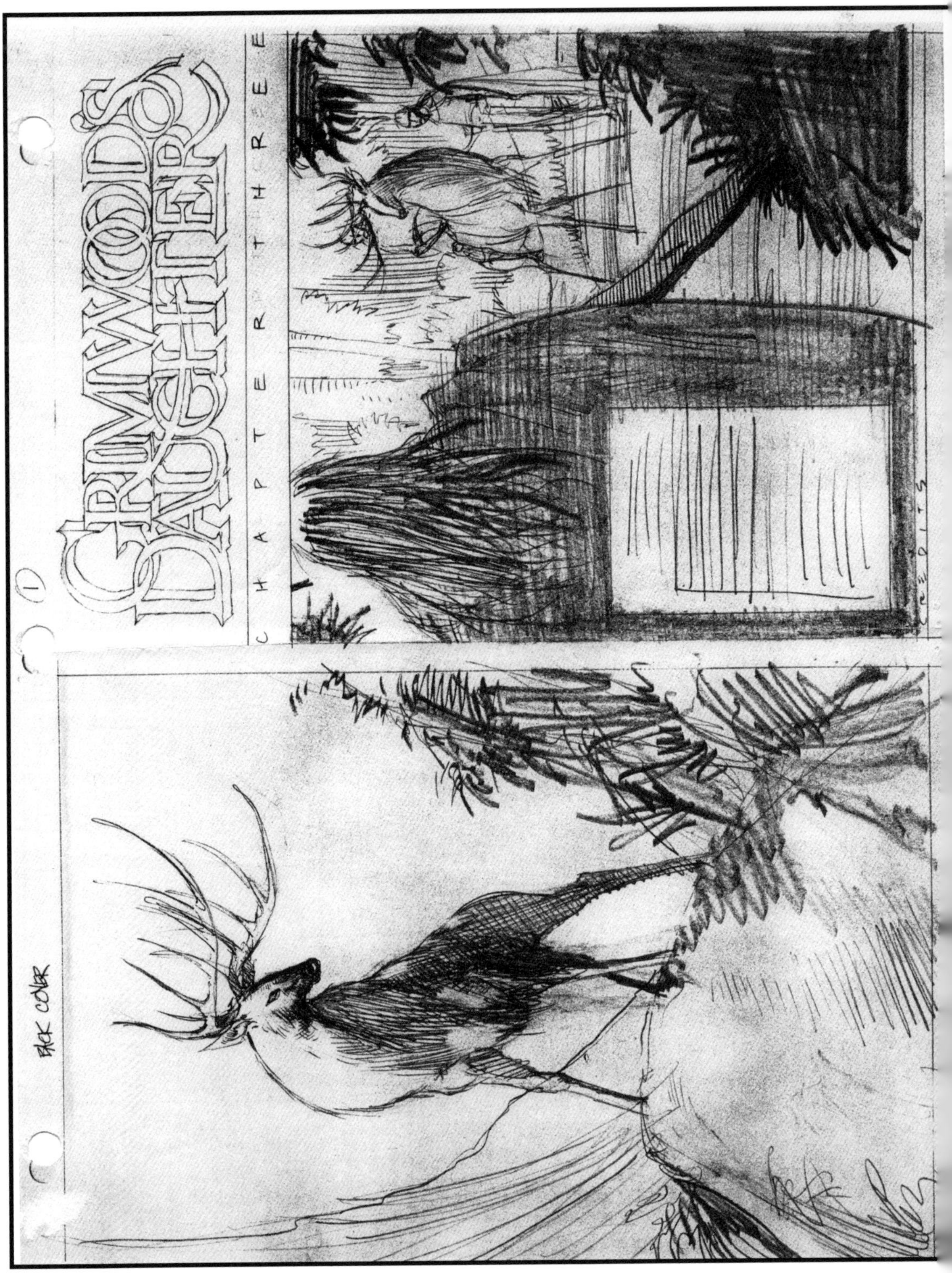
BACK COVER
GRIMWOOD'S DAUGHTER
CHAPTER THREE
CREDITS

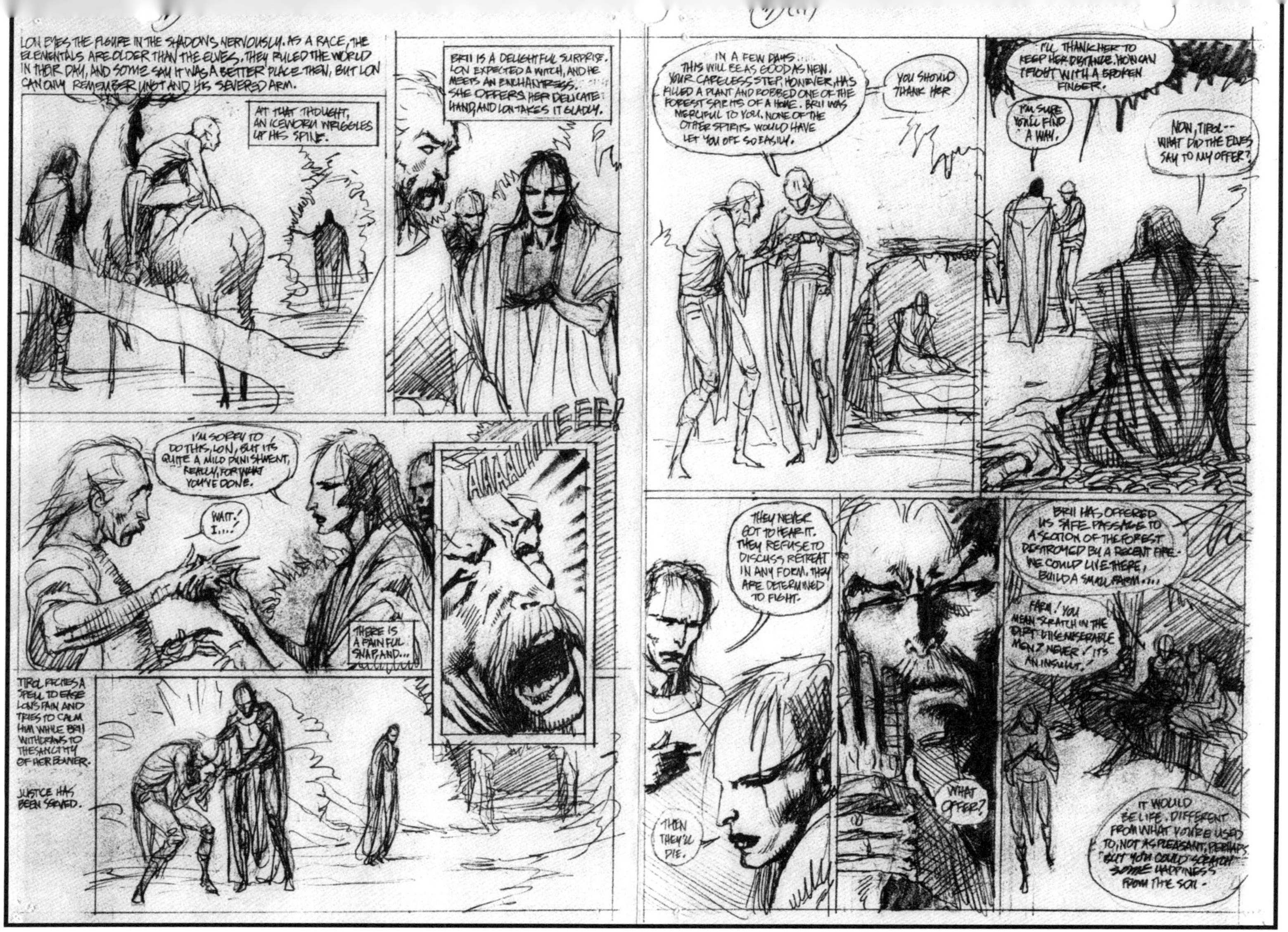
LON EYES THE FIGURE IN THE SHADOWS NERVOUSLY. AS A RACE, THE ELEMENTALS ARE OLDER THAN THE ELVES. THEY RULED THE WORLD IN THEIR DAY, AND SOME SAY IT WAS A BETTER PLACE THEN, BUT LON CAN ONLY REMEMBER UNOT AND HIS SEVERED ARM.
AT THAT THOUGHT, AN ICEWORM WRIGGLES UP HIS SPINE.
BRII IS A DELIGHTFUL SURPRISE. LON EXPECTED A WITCH, AND HE MEETS AN ENCHANTRESS. SHE OFFERS HER DELICATE HAND, AND LON TAKES IT GLADLY.
I'M SORRY TO DO THIS, LON, BUT IT'S QUITE A MILD PUNISHMENT, REALLY, FOR WHAT YOU'VE DONE.
WAIT! I...!
THERE IS A PAINFUL SNAP, AND...
AAAAAIIIEEEE!
TIROL RECITES A SPELL TO EASE LON'S PAIN AND TRIES TO CALM HIM WHILE BRII WITHDRAWS TO THE SANCTITY OF HER BOWER.
JUSTICE HAS BEEN SERVED.
IN A FEW DAYS THIS WILL BE AS GOOD AS NEW. YOUR CARELESS STEP, HOWEVER, HAS KILLED A PLANT AND ROBBED ONE OF THE FOREST SPIRITS OF A HOME. BRII WAS MERCIFUL TO YOU. NONE OF THE OTHER SPIRITS WOULD HAVE LET YOU OFF SO EASILY.
YOU SHOULD THANK HER
I'LL THANK HER TO KEEP HER DISTANCE. HOW CAN I FIGHT WITH A BROKEN FINGER.
YOU'LL FIND A WAY.
NOW, TIROL-- WHAT DID THE ELVES SAY TO MY OFFER?
THEY NEVER GOT TO HEAR IT. THEY REFUSE TO DISCUSS RETREAT IN ANY FORM. THEY ARE DETERMINED TO FIGHT.
THEN THEY'LL DIE.
WHAT OFFER?
BRII HAS OFFERED US SAFE PASSAGE TO A SECTION OF THE FOREST DESTROYED BY A RECENT FIRE. WE COULD LIVE THERE, BUILD A SMALL FARM...
FARM! YOU MEAN SCRATCH IN THE DIRT LIKE MISERABLE MEN? NEVER! IT'S AN INSULT!
IT WOULD BE LIFE, DIFFERENT FROM WHAT YOU'RE USED TO, NOT AS PLEASANT, PERHAPS. BUT YOU COULD SCRATCH SOME HAPPINESS FROM THE SOIL -

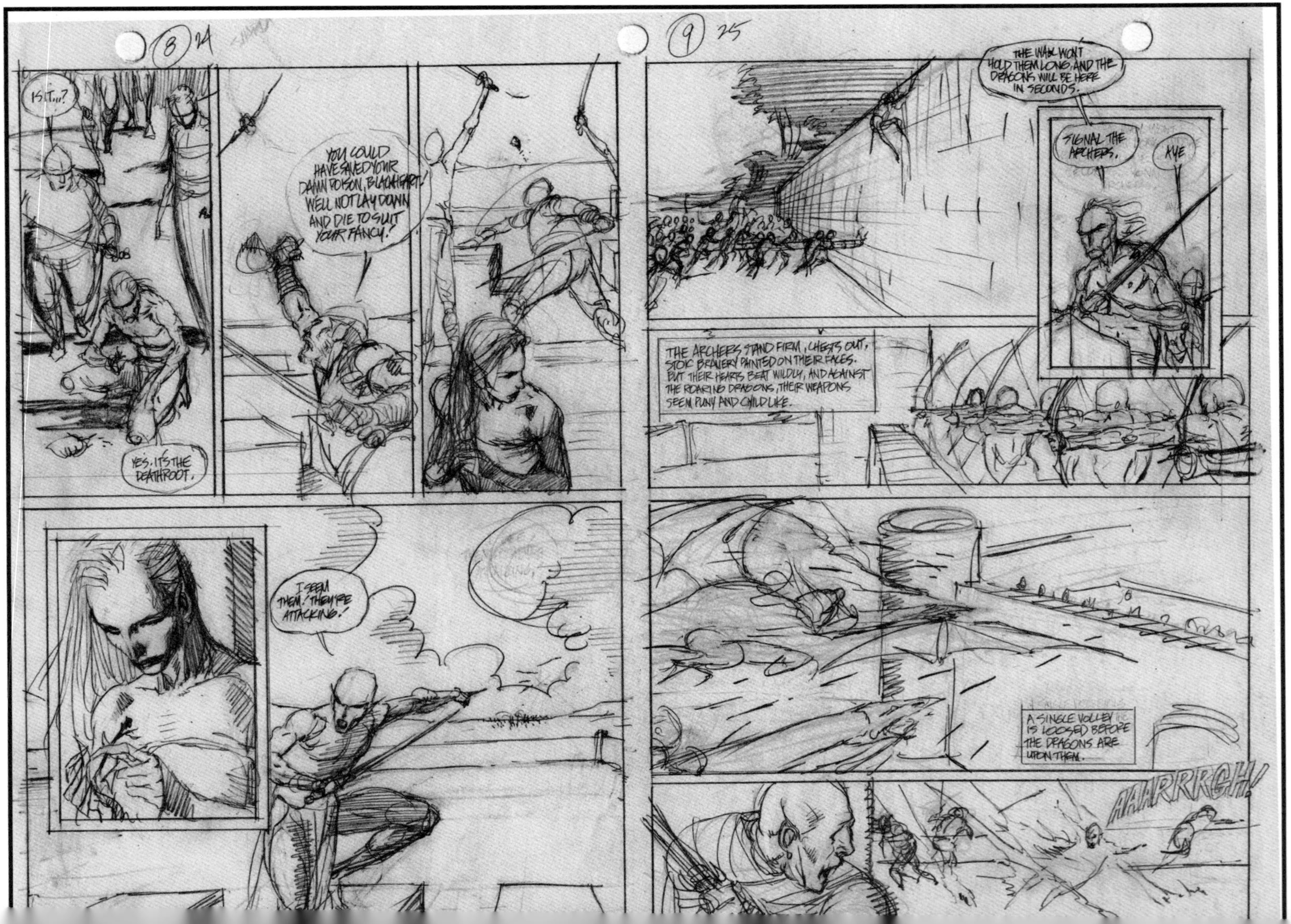
8 24
IS IT...?
YES. IT'S THE DEATHROOT.
YOU COULD HAVE SAVED YOUR DAMN POISON, BLACKHEART! WE'LL NOT LAY DOWN AND DIE TO SUIT YOUR FANCY!
I SEEM THEM! THEY'RE ATTACKING!
9 25
THE WALL WON'T HOLD THEM LONG, AND THE DRAGONS WILL BE HERE IN SECONDS.
SIGNAL THE ARCHERS.
AYE
THE ARCHERS STAND FIRM, CHESTS OUT, STOIC BRAVERY PAINTED ON THEIR FACES. BUT THEIR HEARTS BEAT WILDLY, AND AGAINST THE ROARING DRAGONS, THEIR WEAPONS SEEM PUNY AND CHILD LIKE.
A SINGLE VOLLEY IS LOOSED BEFORE THE DRAGONS ARE UPON THEM.
AAARRRGH!

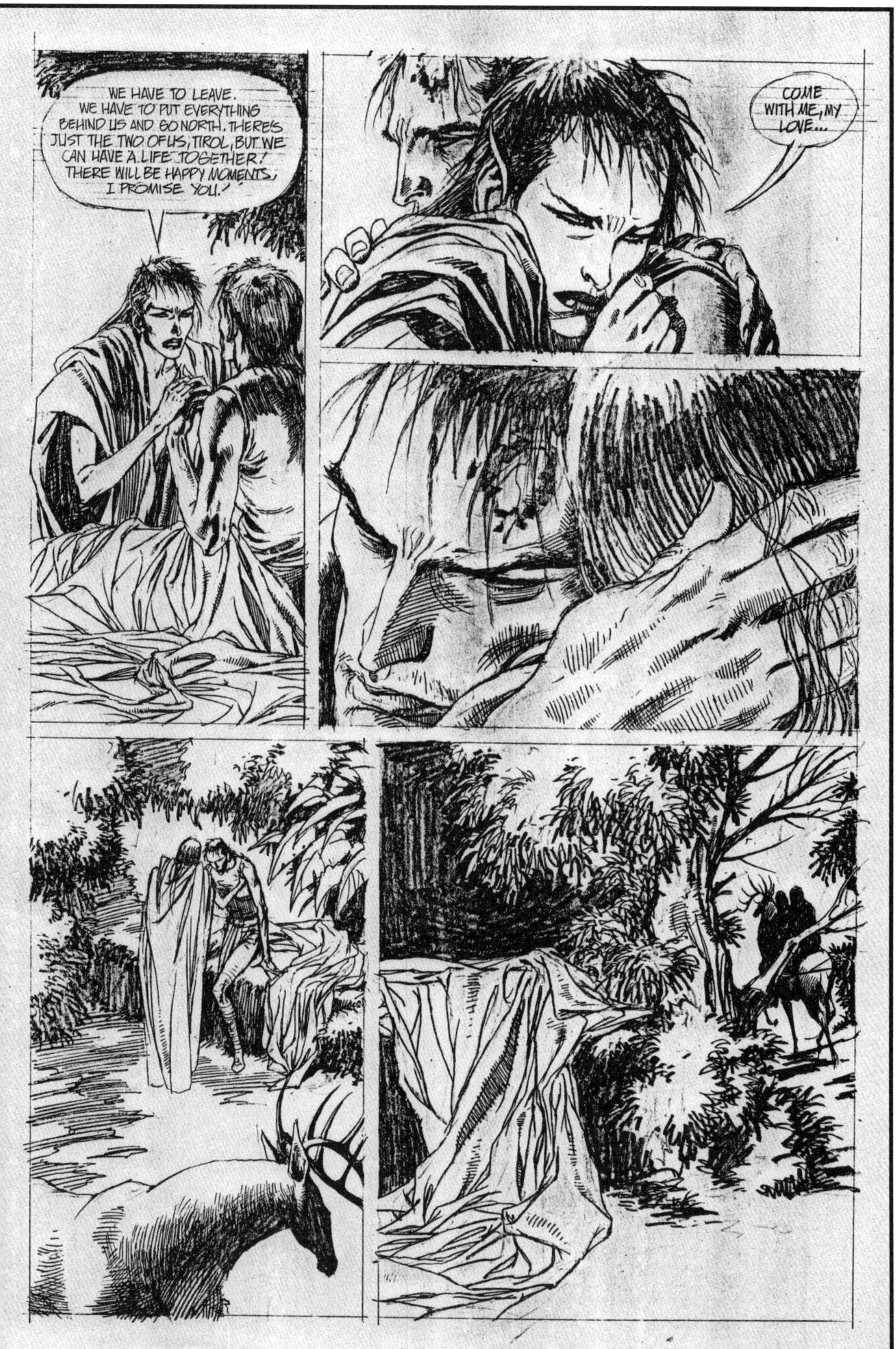
WE HAVE TO LEAVE. WE HAVE TO PUT EVERYTHING BEHIND US AND GO NORTH. THERE'S JUST THE TWO OF US, TIROL, BUT WE CAN HAVE A LIFE TOGETHER! THERE WILL BE HAPPY MOMENTS, I PROMISE YOU!
COME WITH ME, MY LOVE...
FIVE

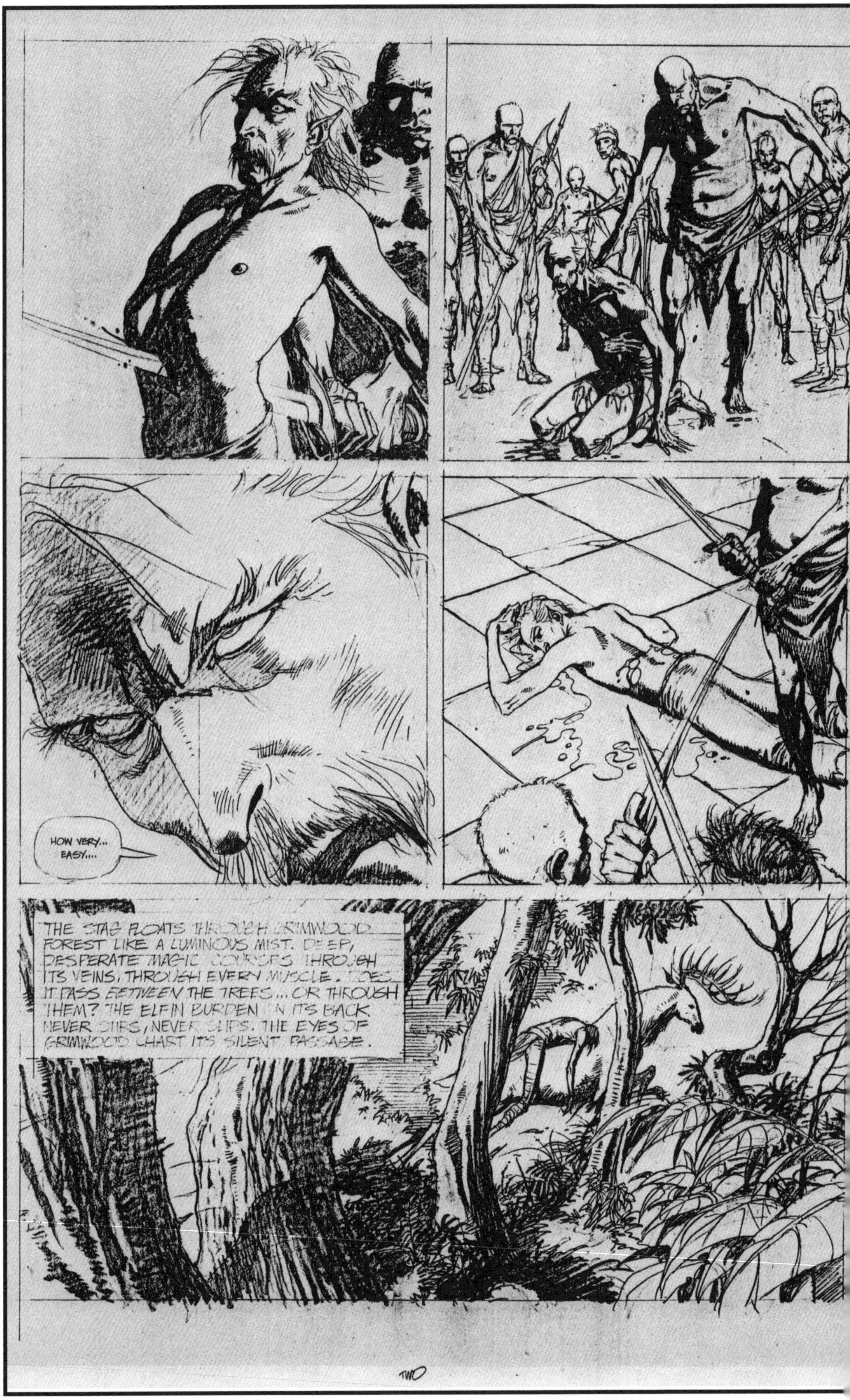
HOW VERY... EASY....
THE STAG FLOATS THROUGH GRIMWOOD FOREST LIKE A LUMINOUS MIST. DEEP, DESPERATE MAGIC COURSES THROUGH ITS VEINS, THROUGH EVERY MUSCLE. DOES IT PASS BETWEEN THE TREES... OR THROUGH THEM? THE ELFIN BURDEN ON ITS BACK NEVER STIRS, NEVER SLIPS. THE EYES OF GRIMWOOD CHART ITS SILENT PASSAGE.
TWO

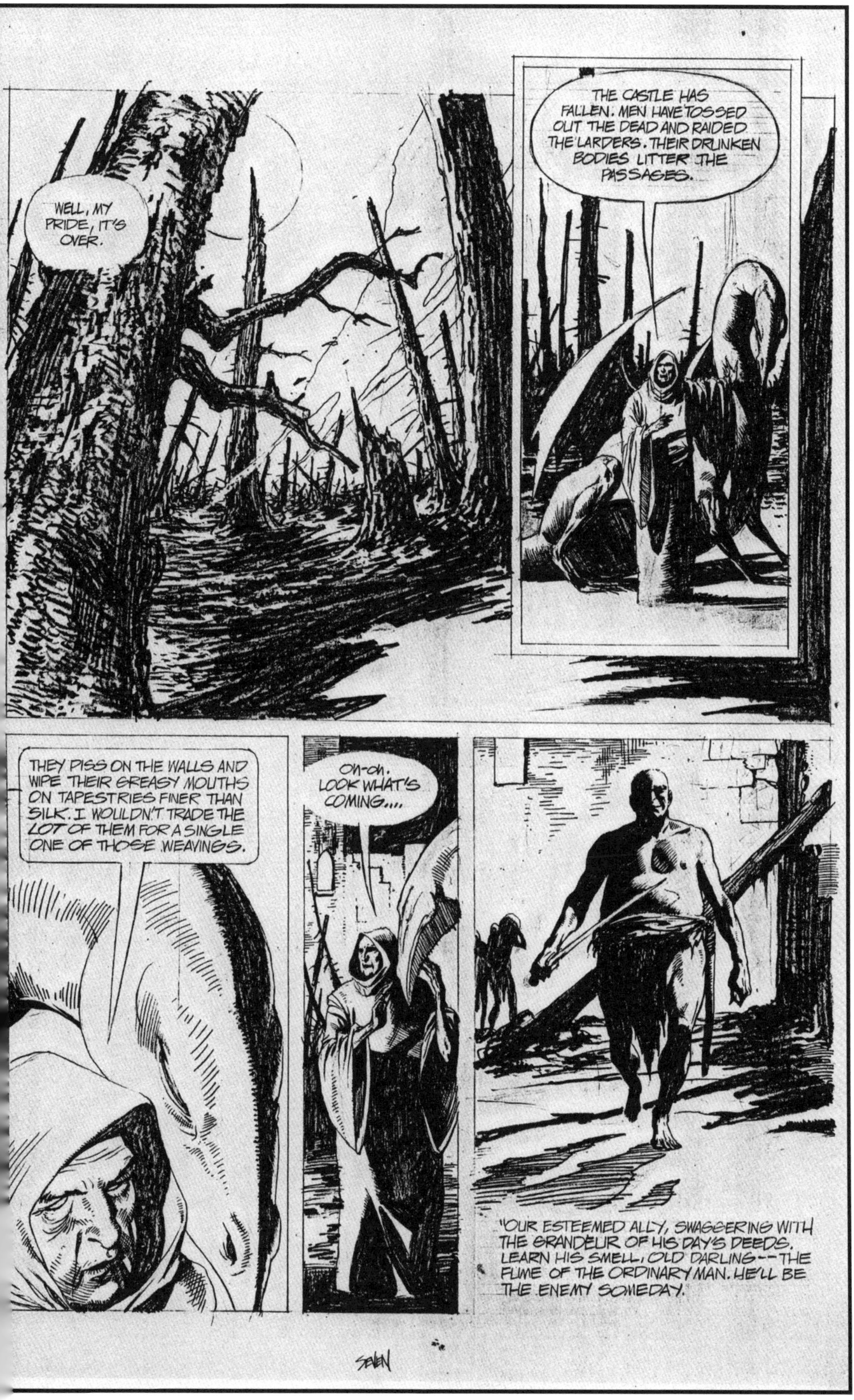
WELL, MY PRIDE, IT'S OVER.
THE CASTLE HAS FALLEN. MEN HAVE TOSSED OUT THE DEAD AND RAIDED THE LARDERS. THEIR DRUNKEN BODIES LITTER THE PASSAGES.
THEY PISS ON THE WALLS AND WIPE THEIR GREASY MOUTHS ON TAPESTRIES FINER THAN SILK. I WOULDN'T TRADE THE LOT OF THEM FOR A SINGLE ONE OF THOSE WEAVINGS.
OH-OH. LOOK WHAT'S COMING....
"OUR ESTEEMED ALLY, SWAGGERING WITH THE GRANDEUR OF HIS DAY'S DEEDS. LEARN HIS SMELL, OLD DARLING-- THE FUME OF THE ORDINARY MAN. HE'LL BE THE ENEMY SOMEDAY.
SEVEN

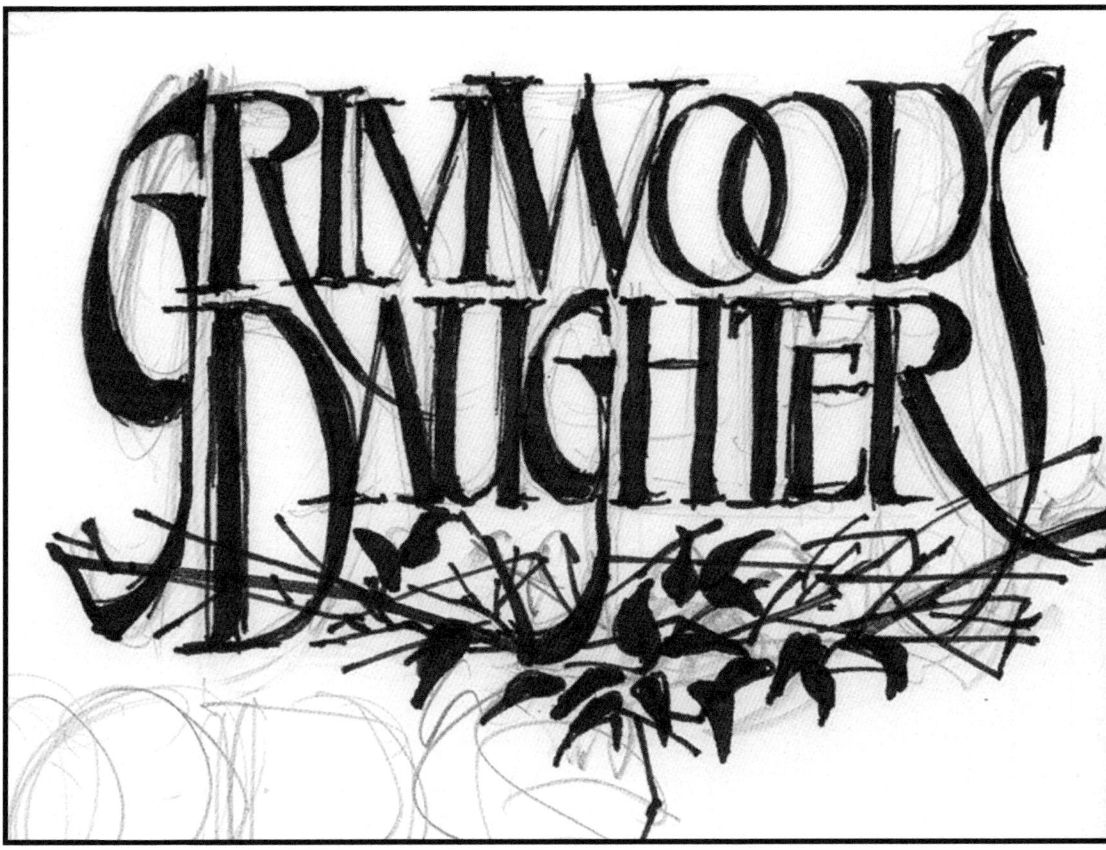
GRIMWOOD'S
DAUGHTER

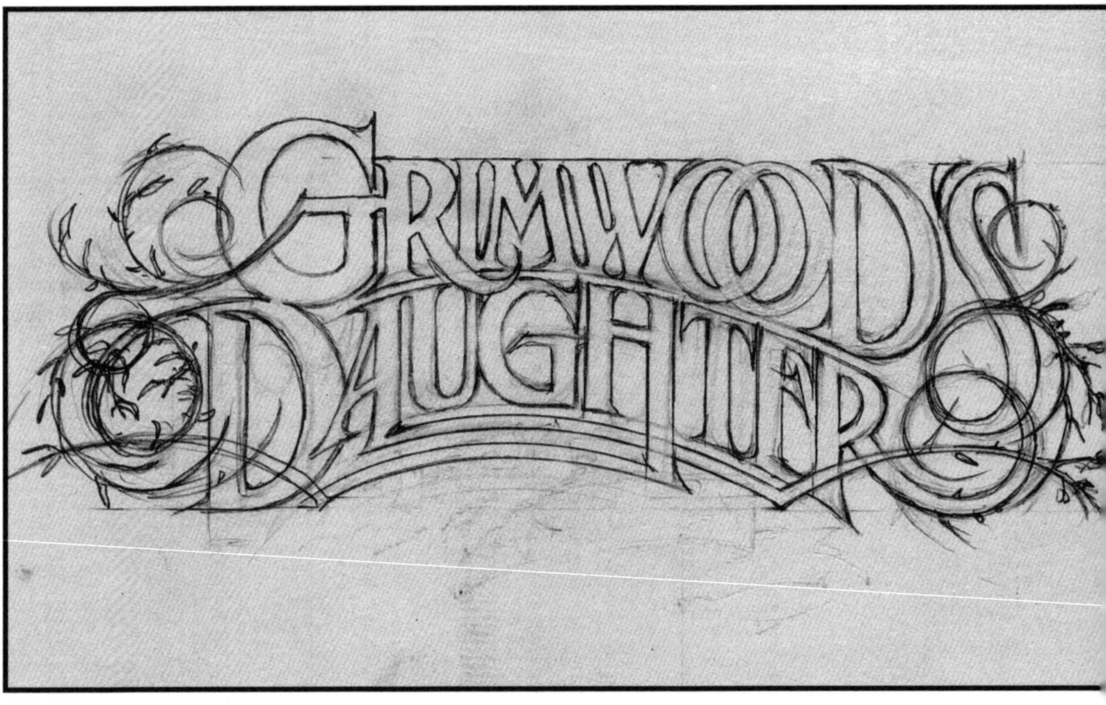
GRIMWOOD'S
DAUGHTER

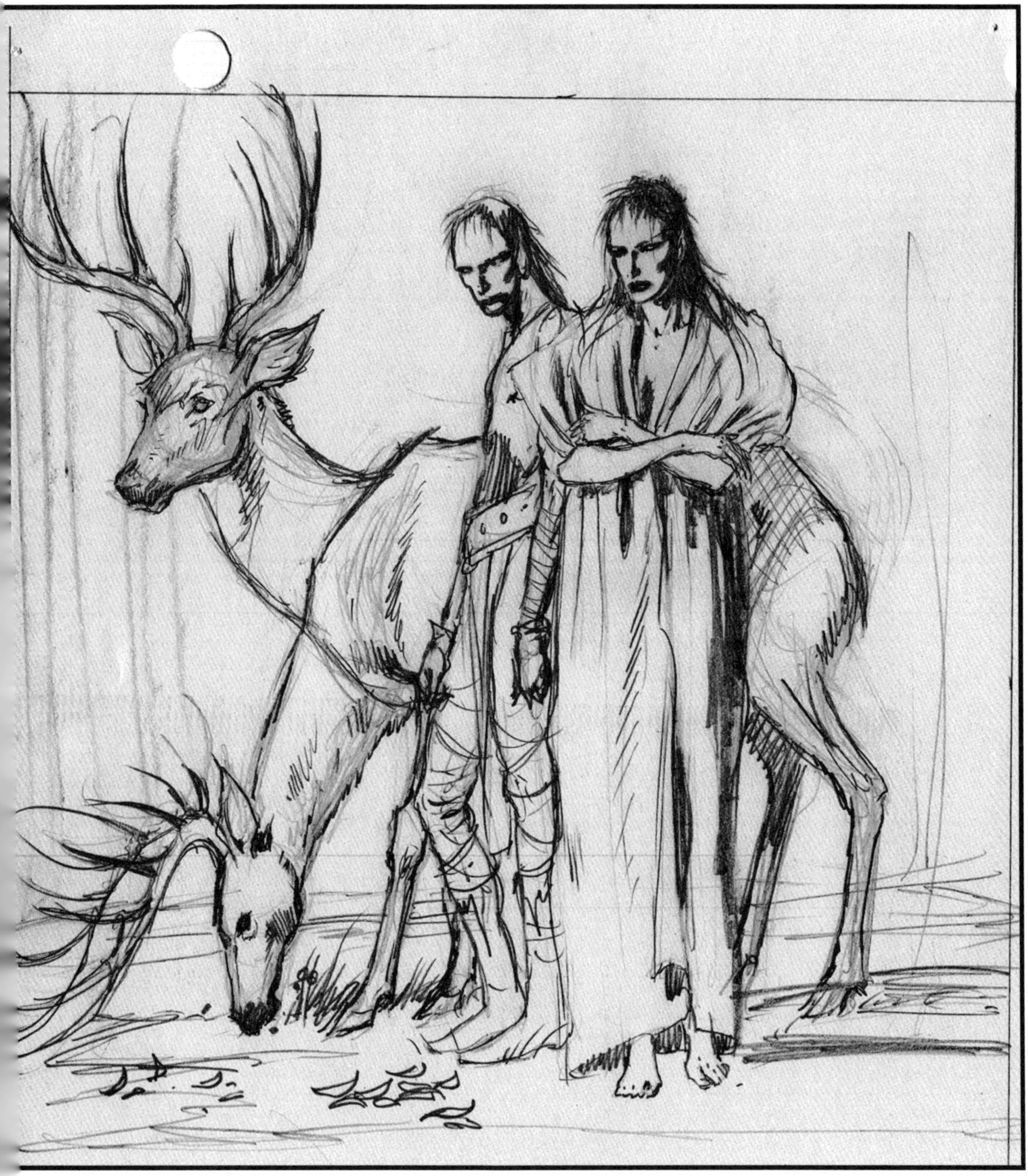

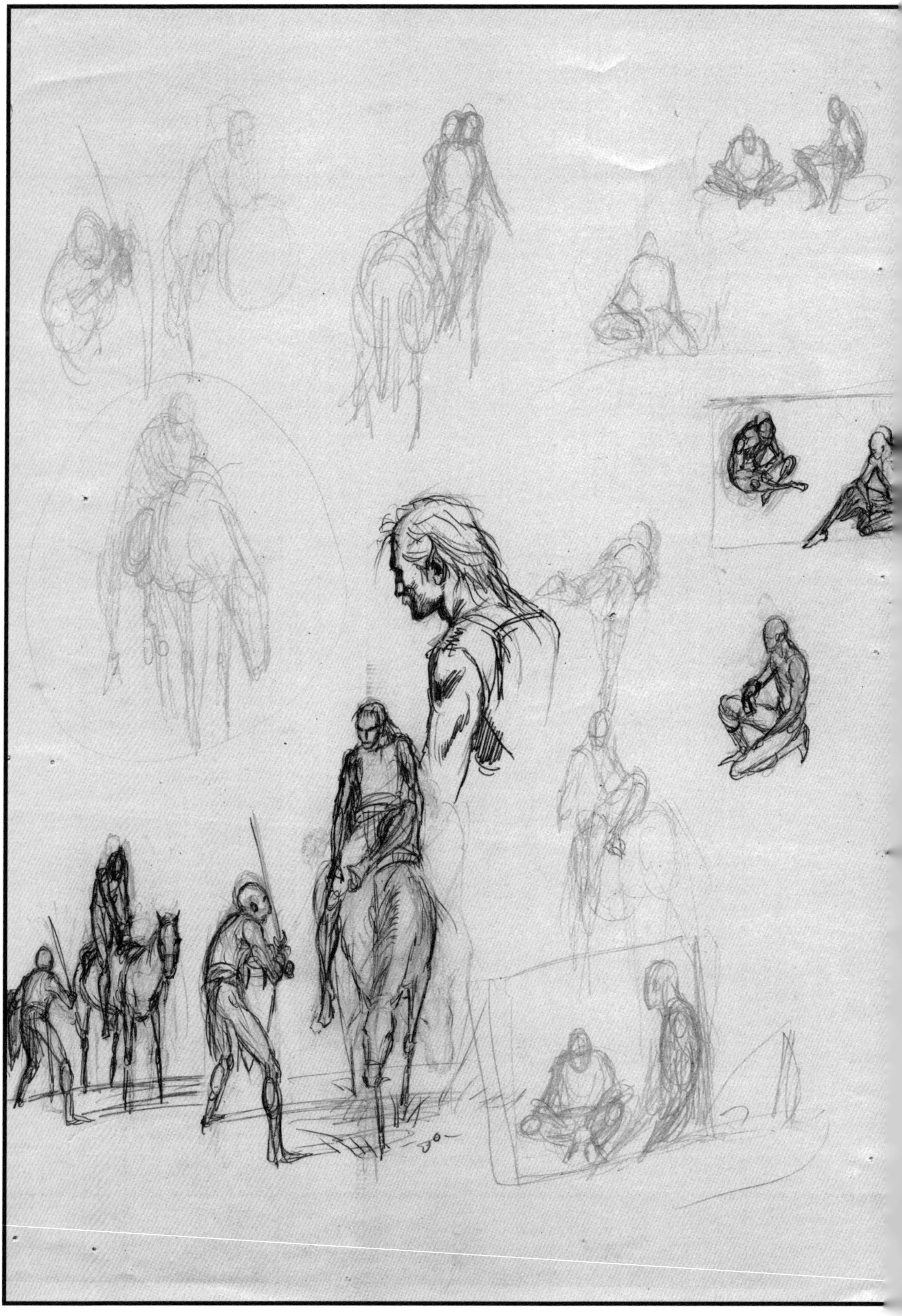

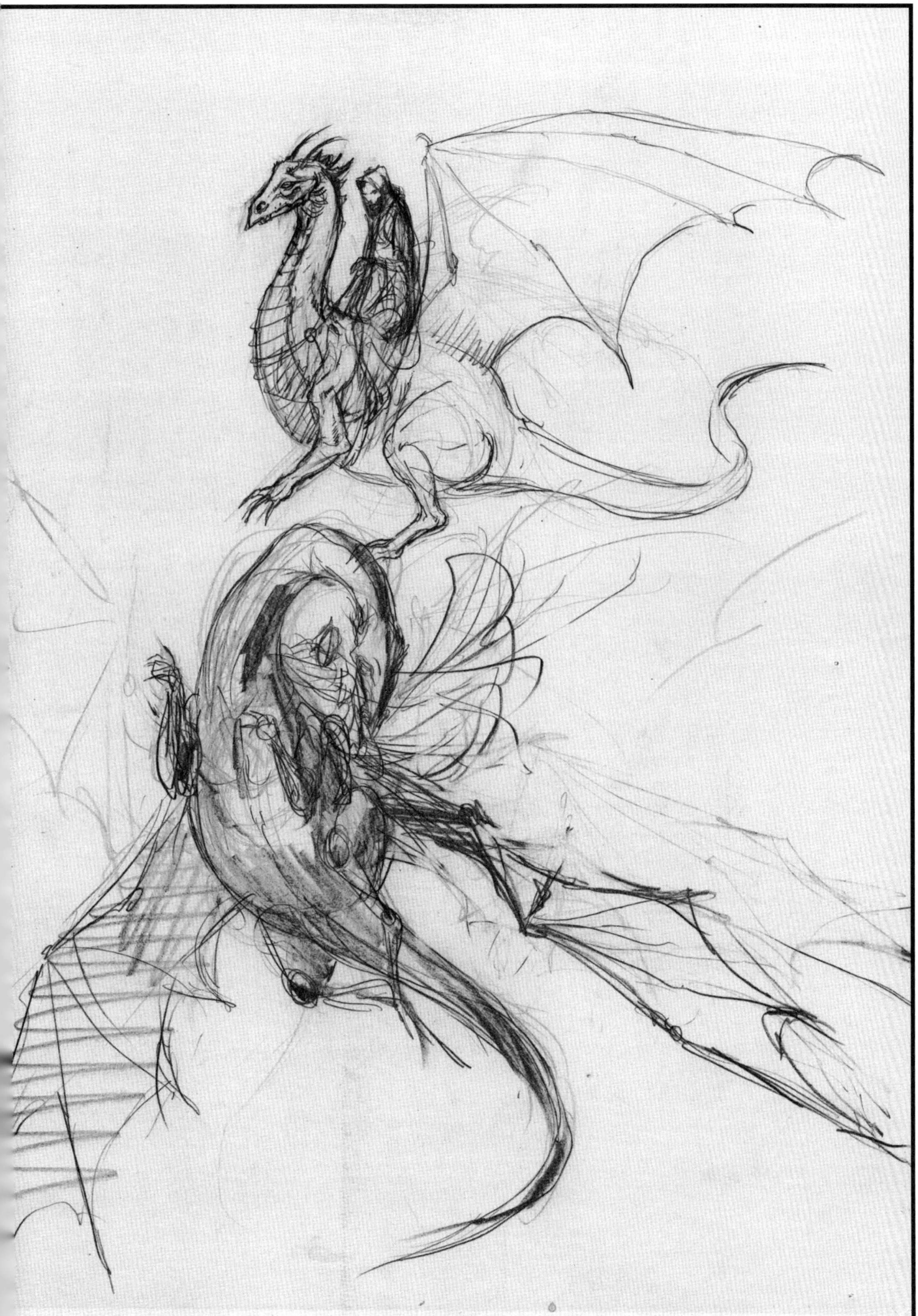

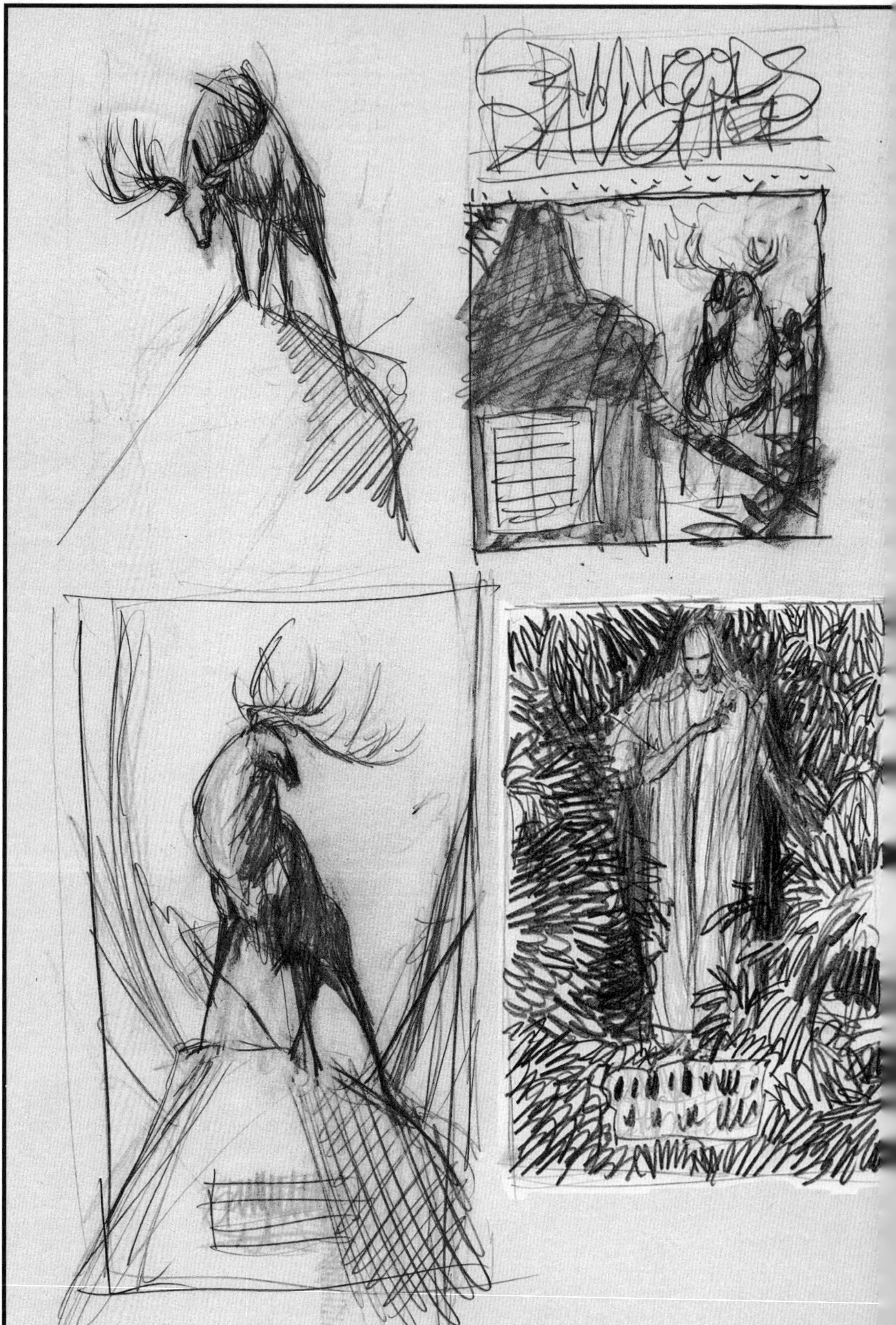